LUTON'S TRANSPORT

A JOURNEY THROUGH TIME

LUTON'S TRANSPORT

A JOURNEY THROUGH TIME

DAVID BEDDALL

PEN & SWORD
TRANSPORT

AN IMPRINT OF PEN & SWORD BOOKS LTD.
YORKSHIRE – PHILADELPHIA

First published in Great Britain in 2022 by
Pen and Sword Transport
An imprint of
Pen & Sword Books Ltd.
Yorkshire - Philadelphia

ISBN 978 1 52675 558 2

Typeset by SJmagic DESIGN SERVICES, India.

Printed and bound in India by Replika Press Pvt. Ltd.

Pen & Sword Books Ltd incorporates the imprints of Pen & Sword Books Archaeology, Atlas, Aviation, Battleground, Discovery, Family History, History, Maritime, Military, Naval, Politics, Railways, Select, Transport, True Crime, Fiction, Frontline Books, Leo Cooper, Praetorian Press, Seaforth Publishing, Wharncliffe and White Owl.

For a complete list of Pen & Sword titles please contact

PEN & SWORD BOOKS LIMITED
47 Church Street, Barnsley, South Yorkshire, S70 2AS, England
E-mail: enquiries@pen-and-sword.co.uk
Website: www.pen-and-sword.co.uk

or

PEN AND SWORD BOOKS
1950 Lawrence Rd, Havertown, PA 19083, USA
E-mail: Uspen-and-sword@casematepublishers.com
Website: www.penandswordbooks.com

FSC
www.fsc.org

MIX
Paper from
responsible sources
FSC® C016779

CONTENTS

ACKNOWLEDGEMENTS

I would firstly like to thank my wife Helen for again putting up with my countless hours spent writing the draft for this book. A big thank you also goes to Gary Seamarks, Matt Robinson and Graham Smith for taking the time to read through my drafts and correct anything that needed correcting. They also provided a number of much needed photographs for this project. As always, a big thank you goes to Liam Farrer-Beddall for allowing me to use his photographs. I would also like to thank Nick Doolan, Hazel Richardson, Peter Waller and the Online Transport Archive for providing other photographs. My last thanks go to Roger Warwick for providing a number of maps for inclusion in this book.

INTRODUCTION

Located on the edge of the Chiltern Hills in South Bedfordshire, the town of Luton is most famous for its hat industry. The town also has a rich transport history, being the home of Vauxhall Motors, and is also the home of London Luton Airport. Luton is also located on the Midland main line, running from London St Pancras International to Bedford, Kettering, Nottingham, Derby and Sheffield to name but a few destinations. Brighton and Gatwick Airport can also be reached on the Thameslink line.

Luton has also had a good selection of bus and coach operators since the introduction of the motor bus at the turn of the twentieth century. The town has been home to numerous independent operators of varying sizes, as well as some larger operators such as London Transport, Eastern National and United Counties. The Centrebus Group also established a successful garage in the town, going from strength to strength. The establishment of Luton Airport has also seen an influx of express coach services from around the United Kingdom, as well as small operations linking the car parks with the terminal building, and Luton town centre with the airport.

The first bus service commenced operation in Luton in 1901 when a horse-drawn bus was purchased by a Mr Jabez Cain of Lilley. The vehicle was used to operate a route along Leagrave Road, with the horses being stabled at Holly Tree Farm, Leagrave. The service successfully operated for a number of years, until August 1914, when the horses owned by Mr Cain were requisitioned by the military, leading to the withdrawal of the service. It was replaced by a similar route operated by a Mr William Burnage, using a car similar to a taxi-cab rather than a bus.

1905 saw the first motor bus route in Bedfordshire commence operation, this being in the Luton area. It coincided with the opening of the tram depot at Wardown Park. At this time, a motor bus was operated between the park and the Town Square by a company called Commer Cars Ltd. This operation did not last very long.

An attempt at linking the neighbouring towns of Luton and Dunstable first took place in July 1905 by London based operator Vanguard. The service was, however, unsuccessful and a second attempt at this link was made later in the year by an operator calling itself the 'Hertfordshire and Bedfordshire Motor Omnibus Company'. It called itself this because it had the intention of extending the service out to St Albans and Watford. However, despite being given backing by Vanguard, nothing further came to fruition. A further two years passed before the next attempt at such a service was tried. A Clarkson steam bus came on loan to the area in September 1907 and was used on this service, which was extended out to the nearby village of Toddington.

The first regular motor bus service commenced operation in Luton in August 1909. This resulted from an original request from Leagrave and Limbury councils for Balfour Beatty to extend the existing tram route from the 'Trough' through to these areas.

This extension was deemed unfeasible and therefore a feeder bus service was introduced by the company. Operated by an eighteen-seat Commer saloon, the route ran to the Three Horseshoes public house in Leagrave; with one journey each way continuing to The Sugar Loaf, Leagrave, where the vehicle was garaged. Originally operating a 30-minute frequency, off-peak journeys were soon dropped to hourly. The service continued operating until March 1913 when Road Motors Limited took the service over. Road Motors had a garage in Manchester Street, Luton, which saw the first and last journeys extend to Luton Town Hall, which was nearby. The horse-bus service mentioned above continued to operate alongside the feeder service.

Five years after the first attempts were made at linking Luton and Dunstable, the first official bus service between the two towns commenced on 31 October 1910, operated by the Dunstable Road Car Company. The service ran from High Street South, Dunstable, to the tram terminus located in Dunstable Road, Luton and was operated in agreement with Balfour Beatty. Soon after, some journeys were extended to Leighton Buzzard and Luton town centre.

The owner of this company, Hugh Jones, went on to form the ill-fated Bedfordshire Road Car Company Limited which commenced operation on 1 April 1911. This new company was formed to purchase a quartet of Thornycroft double-decks from the London General Omnibus Company Limited, placing them into service on the above route. This was unsuccessful, and the service ceased during April 1912. The link was re-established when Road Motors introduced a single Sunday evening service between the two locations. No further services on this corridor operated until May 1920, when the National Omnibus and Transport Company introduced a route between Luton, Dunstable and Leighton Buzzard.

Road Motors Limited was formed in 1910 in Kent. The family and company relocated to Luton in 1912 and from the end of May, commenced a service between Luton, Letchworth and Hitchin. In July the company commenced a Sunday evening service between Luton and Dunstable. Further expansion took place on 17 January 1914 when a Monday to Saturday service was started between Luton and Clophill. Road Motors continued to expand its services in the Luton and Dunstable area, as well as commencing services in north Hertfordshire. In April 1925, Road Motors Ltd was acquired by the National Omnibus Company, with its services being divided between National and the London General Omnibus Company.

David Beddall
Rushden, 2022

Birch Bros. operated a couple of routes into Luton from their base at Henlow Camp. The 212 was inherited from R. Fisher of Gravenhurst in 1938. DEV176 is photographed in Luton operating this service. *D.F. Groome Archive/S.J. Butler Collection*

Court Line Coaches stepped in when London Country withdrew a number of its services in Luton, and to the south of the town. Luton Station finds Plaxton bodied Ford R192 LXD535K, waiting to depart on service 3 for Dunstable. *Graham Smith*

Another vehicle to be operated by Court Line was Duple bodied Ford R192 MXE137K, seen paused in Park Square, Luton. This vehicle was new to the fleet in 1972. The hilly nature of Luton can be seen in the background. *Graham Smith*

An unusual type of vehicle to operate at the airport were three Lex bodied Mercedes-Benz O530G articulated buses. The first of the three, UBH394W, is seen in the photograph below. This vehicle was new in March 1981. *Gary Seamarks*

London Luton Airport has attracted numerous operators over the years, and it would be wrong not to acknowledge the fleet of buses operated by the airport themselves. The airport has operated some more unusual types over the years. One such example is number 17 (G938LFV), an example of the rare Renault PR100 saloon. It is seen loading at the airport bus station. *Gary Seamarks*

Before the construction of Luton Airport Parkway railway station, Luton Airport provided a shuttle service between Luton Midland railway station and Luton Airport. The opening of the Airport Parkway station led to the demise of the service. The late 1990s saw the service operated by a fleet of Ikarus Citibus bodied DAF SB220 saloons, which wore a variety of advertisements. M836RCP demonstrates this, carrying one for Luton-based Easyjet. *Gary Seamarks*

Luton Airport purchased six East Lancs Millennium bodied DAF SB220 saloons in 2000, arriving with the company in July. They were used on car-park shuttles around the airport. W266CDN represents the type and is seen loading before heading to the long-term car park at the rear of the airport. *Gary Seamarks*

A bus more typically associated with airports is the Cobus. Luton Airport is no exception, operating several of the type airside, leaving them un-registered. Number 6 is seen travelling around the apron. *Liam Farrer-Beddall*

Six former London Mercedes-Benz Citaro G articulated buses are also operated airside, having been converted to have doors on the off-side. Former Arriva London MA38 (BX04NEF), now known as Luton's 17, shows off this conversion. It is again seen on the apron of the airport. *Liam Farrer-Beddall*

As mentioned above, Luton has been home to a number of independent operators over the years, as well as having a number of operating services into the town. Buffalo Travel of Flitwick operated numerous contracts and services in Bedfordshire, including a handful into the Luton and Dunstable area. One such route was the 34 between Luton and Dunstable. EAV810V, a Duple bodied Volvo B58 new to Whippet Coaches of Fenstanton, Cambridgeshire, is seen departing Luton on route 34 bound for Dunstable. *Gary Seamarks*

Above: **One of** Luton's most notable independents was Seamarks. The company operated a number of contracts in Luton and Bedfordshire, along with some stage-carriage work. Plaxton Paramount bodied Volvo B10M B544BMH was new to the company in February 1985. It shows off the simplistic livery applied to the fleet. *Gary Seamarks*

Opposite above: **During the** 1990s, Hatfield based Universitybus Ltd (later Uno) introduced a service between Luton and Hatfield, numbering it the 636. Marshall bodied Dennis Dart N424ENM is seen heading back to Hatfield wearing the white and grey livery of Universitybus Ltd. *Gary Seamarks*

Opposite below: **The service** was relaunched in April 2018 as the 'Dragonfly', being extended southwards from Hatfield to Cockfosters. The new service runs via Harpenden, Hatfield and Potters Bar and replaced a service operated by Uno between Luton and Hatfield. A fleet of six MCV eVoRa bodied Volvo B8RLEs were purchased for this new route, which were applied with route branding. 364 (LF18AWR) is seen at Luton Interchange showing off the route branding. *Liam Farrer-Beddall*

CHAPTER ONE
LUTON CORPORATION 1908–1969

This section is designed to show how Luton Corporation, both the tramway and buses, contributed to the development and expansion of Luton's public transport network between 1908 and 1969. The idea of a tramway system for Luton was first discussed in May 1900. It was outlined from the outset that the system would be an electric tramway. The initial proposal was deferred until 1901, when the Luton, Dunstable and District Light Railway scheme was put forward to Luton town council. This scheme proposed a route running from Luton through to Dunstable and Houghton Regis, along with a service running from New Bedford Road in the north of the Luton Borough boundary to New Trapps Lane in the south, passing under the railway bridges to access the town centre. This scheme, after lengthy discussions, was rejected by Luton town council. After a number of altered proposals, 1902 saw further opposition from the Great Northern Railway who operated trains between Luton and Dunstable North.

After a number of other proposals, November 1904 saw an application made to parliament for a Tramways Provisional Order, which was granted. This formed the 'Luton Tramways Order Confirmation Act, 1905'. Construction finally commenced on 7 October 1907. After construction was complete, trials took place on the night of 14 February 1908, with a tramcar running over the section of route between Park Street and Wardown Park. The Luton Tramway officially opened on 21 February 1908. Three routes were operated by a fleet of twelve tramcars, the routes being as follows:

Park Square – Dunstable Road
Town Hall – Round Green
London Road – Wardown Park

Balfour, Beatty and Company took over the lease of the tramway from Luton Corporation in May 1909 and continued to operate the network until 21 February 1923. The takeover by Luton Corporation saw a significant improvement to the service provided on the network.

The Coronation of George V in 1910 was commemorated by the company. Tramcars were decorated both inside and out, with red, white and blue drapes being hung at the windows in the lower saloon. The company also applied Union flags on both sides near to the fleet names.

April 1914 saw some route changes. The Dunstable Road service was extended from the Park Square terminus to Bailey Street. This replaced the section of the Round Green service, which was subsequently cut back to terminate at Luton Town Hall.

The outbreak of the First World War saw services begin to suffer. A number of tramcars were deemed unserviceable, many of which were undergoing long-term repair. This was hindered by staff shortages at the time. To add to this, on 28 December 1916, tramcar 8 was involved in a serious accident. It left the tracks at the bottom of the hill in Midland Road and ran into a traction pole and a brick wall, injuring seven people. This took No. 8 out of service for around eighteen months.

Plans were considered by the local council to extend the routes and replace the trams with trolleybuses and motor buses but nothing originally came of this. In 1930, the local authority was approached by the Eastern National Omnibus Company to acquire the services for a price of £64,000, but not the tram network itself. Local objection to this plan led to the matter being referred to the Ministry of Transport, who declined this offer.

The trams on the London Road to Wardown Park and Dunstable to Wardown Park routes were replaced by Luton Corporation's first motor buses, these taking over the route from 1 March 1932. Nine Duple bodied Daimler CH6 saloons arrived with Luton Corporation in February to operate these routes.

The introduction of a new service between Luton Library and Round Green was introduced in April 1932, being extended to serve Stopsley once an hour. Soon after, Luton Corporation were successful in winning contracts to operate services to both the Vauxhall and Electrolux factories in the town starting in the summer. By October, a circular service had been introduced serving Russell Rise and Hart Lane.

The once an hour extension of the Round Green service to Stopsley became permanent in March 1933. 1933 was a busier year for the Corporation, with eleven new and ten second-hand buses entering the fleet.

Since Luton Corporation commenced motor bus operation, they were keen to expand their operations into areas of Luton such as Stopsley, Biscot Road, Leagrave and the outer parts of New Bedford Road and Dunstable Road. At this time, the Eastern National Omnibus Company were providing services to these areas. However, in the autumn of 1932, the prospect of expansion into these areas took a step forward. The name A.F. England is one that will reoccur in this book. England was a prolific operator in the Luton and Dunstable areas, owning companies named XL Services, Blue Bird and Union Jack. In October 1932, A.F. England was looking to sell his various bus interests. Under the name Blue Bird, England operated a number of routes within the Borough of Luton, to the north of the town centre. It was this operation that caught the attention of Luton Corporation; this would allow them to expand into the areas mentioned. However, England would only sell all three companies, not individual ones. Since the operating area of these three operations exceeded the boundaries of Luton Borough, objection was initially met from Eastern National regarding a number of routes to areas such as Leighton Buzzard, Pegsdon, Dunstable and Whipsnade Zoo. Under the Midnight Agreement, detailed in the Eastern National section of this book, it was agreed that both Luton Corporation and Eastern National could expand their operations within Luton, with Luton Corporation being allowed to operate services outside of the borough boundary, to serve Dunstable, Houghton Regis and Warden Hill (Bramington Turn). The original offer made was £21,000, which included fourteen vehicles and one chassis, with the Union Jack (Luton) Omnibus Co. Ltd name to remain with A.F. England. The sale was subject to approval by the East Midland Traffic Commissioner. The price was reduced to £17,250 after the Midnight Agreement was finalised. This price included ten vehicles, and the routes within Luton, Dunstable, Houghton Regis and Warden Hill. The new licences took effect from February 1933, the acquisition taking place on 23 March. A.F. England used the Union Jack (Luton) Omnibus Co. Ltd name to acquire further bus operations in the Bedford area. England returned to the Luton area on 27 March 1933, when he acquired the business of Lamb Bros. 'Renown Service', who operated a route between Luton and Flamstead.

Under the acquisition, the former Blue Bird garage on New Bedford Road was rented by Luton Corporation Transport. The yard was shared with Union Jack. The existing bus garage premises at Park Street, Luton underwent modification at this time. Doors at the rear were installed, opening on to a new, unsurfaced yard with additional access provided by a new unsurfaced drive beside the transport offices. An additional garage building was also constructed, this being done during 1934. This allowed Luton Corporation to leave the New Bedford Road site in April 1934. December 1933 saw the introduction of route numbers, helping to clarify which service the vehicle was operating.

March 1937 saw the introduction of a new route numbered 22. The service ran between Park Square and Chaul End Lane.

The following month, the company commenced operation of a new contract providing a service for workers of the Percival Aircraft factory at Luton Airport. At this time, the access roads to the airport were small and therefore a full-sized bus could not fit and a smaller Bedford saloon was purchased.

The location of the Vauxhall Motors factory and Luton Airport in the town drew attention to Luton from the Germans during the Second World War. Vauxhall at the time were building Churchill tanks and other vehicles for the war effort. As a result, Luton took a number of hits from enemy action. Luton Corporation itself took two direct hits during 1940. The first took place on 30 August when a bomb struck Park Street garage killing two members of staff and destroying bus number 19. The second, more severe attack, took place on 22 September when the offices and garage building were severely damaged along with forty-six Luton Corporation vehicles.

A number of operators around the United Kingdom during the war experimented with running buses using producer gas in a bid to save fuel. Luton Corporation was no exception with single-deck number 5 being converted for such an experiment. It was done by the addition of a trailer. Luton as a town is quite a hilly area and this led to the failure of the experiment. The vehicle was under-powered to tackle climbing these hills, and the experiment was abandoned.

July 1944 saw Luton Corporation step in to help London Transport. At this time the latter company saw a demand for additional morning journeys on routes 337 and 376A into Dunstable from Studham, Whipsnade and Kensworth, a demand with which they could not cope. Luton Corporation provided an additional weekday peak-time service between Luton and Studham, running via Dunstable, Kensworth and Whipsnade Cross Roads, taking route number 25 initially before later being added as an extra journey to route 5.

The Summer of 1945 also saw a twice-weekly visitors' service linking Dunstable with Ashridge Memorial Hospital commence operation by London Transport. Luton Corporation Transport offered to provide the facility, but London Transport considered this was now within their resources and the new service appeared as Wednesday and Sunday route 352A (Dunstable-Dagnall -Ashridge Memorial Hospital).

An arrangement, known as the Luton and District Transport Agreement, was reached between Luton Corporation and Eastern National on 11 October 1948, further details of which can be found under that heading. This was caused by the post-war housing boom which saw the Luton and Dunstable areas expand, causing problems for both operators to extend and alter existing services to provide transport links for these new housing areas. The Traffic Commissioner suggested that both concerns work together, after they both submitted competing applications for services. The new initiative commenced on 2 January 1949.

Under the agreement, Luton Corporation routes 2 and 3 were joined and extended. They were renumbered to 1 (Cutenhoe Road-Seymour Avenue) and 1A (Cutenhoe Road-Hockwell Ring). Route 4 was combined with Eastern National's route 55 to form a new, jointly operated service 4 running between Skimpot (Dunstable Road), Luton (Park Square) and Stopsley Green. Routes 5, 6 and 7 remained unaltered. Route 8 retained its original route number under the agreement but was rerouted to run from Bradgers Hill Road to Farley Hill Estate, Whipperly Way. Route 9 also retained its original number but was changed to operate from Russell Rise to Biscot Mill. Routes 11 and 11A were joined with Eastern National's route 63, and ran between Warren Road, Luton (Bridge Street) and Stopsley, Rochester Avenue. Service 12 was another route that remained unaltered, as did routes 17, 23 and 24.

Luton Corporation's route 15 was withdrawn, but the number was reused for a works service between Vauxhall and Farley Hill, incorporating the former route 18. Another joint route was the 52D, this being an amalgamation of Luton Corporation's routes 21 and 22 and Eastern National's route 52D. The new route ran from Chaul End Lane to Vauxhall and Luton Airport, running via Hart Lane, Round Green and Stopsley.

The period between 1950 and 1952 was a quiet one in terms of vehicles. No new vehicles were taken into stock during this time. The only vehicle movement of note was the loan of an MCCW bodied Leyland Olympic for which the registration is unknown. The vehicle was loaned from Leyland Motors in May 1950 and used for one week in service.

Luton Corporation's involvement in the Luton to Studham service, route 5, introduced in July 1944 to assist London Transport along this corridor, ceased on 31 July 1950. It was at this time that London Transport extended the peak hour journeys on their service 376A to operate between Studham, Whipsnade and Dunstable.

A second phase of the Luton and District Transport agreement came into effect from September 1951. At this time, route 53B was introduced to run between Luton, Dunstable and Whipsnade Zoo. This became jointly operated with Eastern National. This was also the case for route 54, which commenced operation at the same time. The full route operated between Luton, Toddington and Ampthill but Luton Corporation was only involved in the section between Luton and Toddington. From this date, Luton Corporation and Eastern National also joined forces to operate route 56 between Park Square and Limbury, Biscott Mill. Route 57 combined Luton Corporation route 13 and Eastern National's route 57 and ran from Luton Station to Leagrave and Hockwell Ring. The final route to be introduced was the 59, another jointly operated route with Eastern National. It operated between Luton and Sundon.

The original Tramway garage at Park Street became a bit cramped during the 1960s due to the expansion of the company. Therefore, a new garage facility was opened at Kingsway, opening in April 1963. The town also received a bus station in August 1964, lasting five years before an alternative site was found and opened.

The expiration of the Luton & District Transport agreement in January 1970, along with financial trouble, led Luton Corporation to begin negotiations with United Counties as early as 1968. An offer was made in October 1969 and operations of Luton Corporation were taken over by United Counties on 4 January 1970.

UEC tramcar 1 is seen stopped on Bedford Road, Luton heading for the Town Hall. *Barry Cross Collection/Online Transport Archive*

As the wording on the photograph suggests, tramcar 7 is captured passing the Public Library in Luton whilst heading towards London Road. *Barry Cross Collection/Online Transport Archive*

High Town Road, Luton, Luton.

High Town Road, Luton finds tramcar 11 operating the Round Green service. *Barry Cross Collection/Online Transport Archive*

The only single-deck tramcar to be operated by Luton Corporation was acquired from Glasgow Corporation, being cut down from a double-deck tramcar. It is photographed at the depot. *Barry Cross Collection/Online Transport Archive*

1947 and 1948 saw the arrival of a number of Crossley and Leyland double-decks with Luton Corporation. 99 (EBM99) represents the Crossley model, the DD42/3T. *R.L. Wilson/Online Transport Archive*

Toddington Green finds Luton Corporation's Leyland PD2/1 116 (FNM116), a 1948 delivery, when being used on driver training duties. *Graham Smith*

119 (FNM119) is another example of the Leyland PD2/1 operated by Luton Corporation. June 1967 finds the vehicle on layover in Library Road, Luton. Note the lack of route number applied to the destination display. 119 was new to Luton Corporation in April 1948. *Graham Smith*

March 1953 saw the arrival of five Leyland Titan PD2/10 double-decks. The last of the quintet is 128 (LBM128), seen here passing through Market Hill, Luton in April 1969. It is seen heading towards Cutenhoe Road on route 27. *Graham Smith*

138 (MNM138) is the last of a batch of ten Leyland PD2/10 double-decks delivered to Luton Corporation between October 1953 and June 1954. Delivered in June 1954, 138 was the last Leyland bodied vehicle taken into stock by the Corporation. It is seen travelling down Guildford Street, Luton whilst operating a journey on route 11 to Warren Road in April 1968. *Graham Smith*

Hitchin Road, Luton finds 141 (RNM141) travelling towards Stopsley on route 11. 141 formed part of a batch of nine MCCW bodied Leyland Titan PD2/22s delivered to Luton Corporation in October 1956. They subsequently passed to United Counties in 1970. *Graham Smith*

Luton Bus Station finds 171 (171HTM) in May 1969 waiting to depart for Bramingham Lane on route 14. New in July 1963, 171 formed part of a batch of ten East Lancs bodied Albion LR7s new to Luton Corporation during 1963. *Graham Smith*

Five East Lancs bodied Leyland Titan PD2/30s were delivered to Luton Corporation in July and August 1960. Representing this batch is 158 (158ANM) which is seen operating route 11 towards Stopsley. It is captured in November 1969 travelling down Dallow Road. *Graham Smith*

November 1965 saw the arrival of six non-standard Neepsend bodied Dennis Loline II double-decks to the company. Showing off this type is 183 (FXD183C), seen on route 6 towards Luton, about to exit Southwood Road, Dunstable in August 1968. *Graham Smith*

Luton Corporation took stock of a Stratchan bodied Bedford VAM14 in March 1966 from Vauxhall Motors Ltd of Luton. It was operated by the company until July of the same year, operating on a variety of services with the company. It is seen here travelling along George Street, Luton shortly after arriving with the company in March. *Graham Smith*

104 (MXD104E) formed part of the first batch of Bristol RE saloons bodied by ECW to start the conversion of routes in the Luton area to one-person-operation. It is seen here loading in the Priestleys area of Luton in this July 1967 shot. *Graham Smith*

117 (PXE117G) was new to Luton Corporation in February 1969 and formed part of the third batch of Bristol RELL6L saloons to be purchased by the company. It is seen here posing for the camera on Hereford Road, Luton in December 1969. *Graham Smith*

Richmond Hill, Luton finds 121 (UXD121G) en route to the Vauxhall Works in Luton. 121 was the first of a batch of ten ECW bodied Bristol RELL6Ls delivered to the company in 1969, these being the last batch of vehicles delivered new and operated by Luton Corporation. It is seen in April 1969 when only two months old. *Graham Smith*

Luton Corporation's Kingsway garage finds 134 (XXE134H), one of five ECW bodied Bristol LHS6P saloons delivered to the company in late 1969. These vehicles, however, did not enter service with either Luton Corporation or their successor, United Counties. Instead, they went to the National Bus Company who then allocated them to Eastern Counties Omnibus Company who re-registered them with local registration marks. *Graham Smith*

CHAPTER TWO

NATIONAL OMNIBUS COMPANY TO STAGECOACH EAST

A s the title suggests, this section takes a look at the operations of the National Steam Car Company; National Omnibus and Road Transport Company; the Eastern National Omnibus Company Limited; United Counties Omnibus Company and Cambus Ltd operations in the Luton and Dunstable areas. These companies operated within the Eastern Traffic area, an area covering the east, north and west of Luton. National's operations in the Metropolitan Traffic area are explored in the London Connections section.

National Omnibus Company

On 19 June 1909, Thomas Clarkson formed the National Steam Car Company Limited in the Essex town of Chelmsford. The company formed the foundations of the Eastern National Omnibus Company Limited and Western National Omnibus Company Limited.

The company began operations in London in November 1909, running a service between Shepherd's Bush and Westminster, via Marble Arch, Oxford Street and Regent Street. Over the coming years, the company expanded its operations in the capital, with the main focus on the Peckham and Camberwell areas.

The New Central Omnibus Company Limited opened a garage in St Johns Street, Bedford in May 1912. The garage soon passed to the London General Omnibus Company Limited, who traded as the Bedford Motor Omnibus Company Limited. The company operated from this premises for just over two years before St Johns Street was vacated by London General in November 1914, the building being requisitioned by the War Department.

After the First World War, two deals were made between the London General Omnibus Company Limited and the National Steam Car Company Limited. The first deal – and most important for the area included in this section – which was reached between the two companies took place in 1919. Under this deal, National would withdraw operating in the Greater London area, with the garage at Nunhead transferring to London General's control at a time when they had sufficient motorbuses to replace the older Clarkson steam buses. In exchange, National acquired the St Johns Street, Bedford garage, giving the company a free hand to introduce country bus services in Bedfordshire and North Hertfordshire. One condition to this was these services had to remain a distance of at least 20 miles from Charing Cross. London General had a commitment to provide National with an unknown number of surplus AEC B-type double-decks once all had been returned from Army service, this not occurring until 1921-2. National duly took over Bedford garage in August 1919, whilst Nunhead passed to London General in December, when the last National Clarksons were withdrawn from service.

The National Steam Car Company was retitled the National Omnibus & Transport Company in February 1920, and subsequently also expanded at numerous new locations in the West Country.

The expansion of National in Bedford during 1919 was dramatic, using new AEC YC chassis vehicles on which former steam bus double-deck bodies were fitted, usually retaining the former Steam Car livery of off-white. New bus services soon reached Cranfield, Biggleswade, St. Neots, Newport Pagnell, Shefford, Woburn and Leighton Buzzard.

The first attempt to enter the Luton area was made in November 1919 but was deferred by the Luton Borough Watch Committee. Tom Attree was a member of this committee, being a Councillor as well as the proprietor of Luton-based bus operator Road Motors Limited and the deferral worked to Attree's advantage, allowing him to expand his presence in Luton, along with increasing the size of his bus fleet. National was soon granted permission to operate in Luton, and commenced operation over the Easter of 1920, starting a service between Leighton Buzzard and Luton using two motorbuses, initially operated from an outstation in Leighton Buzzard before another was established on Luton Road, Dunstable. A service to Aylesbury was also operated in 1920, but was soon met with competition, leading to its withdrawal. The surplus bus from the loss of this route allowed the company to start up a new service to Leagrave and Dunstable. By the end of the year, a third service between Dunstable and Redbourn had commenced, this later being extended to St Albans. By 1921, National were operating four services in the Luton and Dunstable areas, these being as follows:

16   *Luton – Leagrave – Toddington*
18   *Luton – Dunstable – Leighton Buzzard*
20   *Bedford – Clophill – Luton*
21   *Dunstable – Redbourn – St Albans until June 1921*

Route 20 was the only one of the four to be operated directly from Bedford. Over the coming years, small developments helped the company to expand in the local area. London General approached National about helping them operate a number of services in the area south of Luton, and into Hertfordshire on their behalf, with London General providing the vehicles, and National maintaining them and providing the workforce.

A number of small route developments took place in the Luton and Dunstable area during 1922. A new service, numbered the 3, was introduced in the summer, linking Dunstable with Bedford. The route number had been previously used by National for a route between Bedford and Cranfield, before National withdrew this provision.

Route 16 was withdrawn in 1922 between Luton and Toddington, this being replaced by other services linking Dunstable and Edlesborough.

Service 9c was also introduced in 1922, this being a short-lived route running between Luton and Shefford. The 9c was re-used by National for a route in the Hitchin area, which was also short-lived. The third incarnation of this service was introduced in 1925 for a service running between Luton, Higham Gobion and Hitchin.

1923 saw the introduction of a short service between neighbouring Dunstable and Houghton Regis. The same year saw a new service, the 16A, commence running between Dunstable and Studham. A year later, the route was extended through to Luton.

Several mentions have already been made of Tom Attree and his company Road Motors Limited. In April 1925, the National Omnibus and Transport Company purchased Road Motors for a sum of £65,000. The purchase included a small operation in the Weymouth area of Dorset, which transferred to National a month earlier.

The sale included forty-four buses, along with orders for several new Daimler buses, and a garage in Langley Street, Luton, which at the time of purchase was overcrowded. A garage in Weymouth and a small garage and adjoining cottages in Toddington were also included, along with a new garage in Pixmore Avenue, Letchworth which was under construction at that time. In total, sixteen routes were acquired by National, 2 being in the Weymouth area, the other fourteen in Bedfordshire. Of these, nine were operated in the area under review in this book. These were as follows:

52	*Luton – Hitchin – Letchworth – Norton*
53	*Luton – Leagrave – Dunstable*
54	*Luton – Leagrave – Toddington*
56	*Vauxhall – Luton – Linbury*
57	*Luton – Leagrave*
58	*Luton – Houghton Regis*
59	*Luton – Leagrave – Sundon*
63	*Luton (Memorial) – Dallow Road*
65	*Luton – Stopsley – Ramridge Road*

The closing years of the National Omnibus and Transport Company saw very few route developments take place in the Eastern traffic area, the majority of changes taking place south of Luton. However, in 1926 a new service commenced linking Dunstable with Tebworth, taking up service number 18A.

At the same time, route 16A was renumbered 16 and was extended from Edlesborough to Ivinghoe. The frequency on route 18 (Luton-Leighton Buzzard) was increased, with some trips diverted to serve Tilsworth and Stanbridge. In 1928, the Tebworth section of this service was added to the 3a, running between Harlington, Toddington and Dunstable. At the same time, the frequency of services running between Luton and Bedford were also increased, and a new service between Luton and Clophill, via Greenfield, was introduced, numbered the 20B. A more direct link between Luton and Clophill was provided by route 20A.

National's presence in Luton was increased in March 1929 when the operations of Ideal Motor Coaches Limited of Luton were acquired. The latter operator had been established in the early 1920s by Edward George Salter, with garages being established in both Luton and Dunstable. A pair of Karrier six-wheeled double-deckers were operated by Salter on a service between Dunstable and Edlesborough. Later in its history, the route was jointly operated by National and Ideal.

In August 1929, the National Omnibus and Transport Company acquired the business of Atkinson of Biggleswade, trading as Biggleswade Blue Bus. This significantly expanded National's operations in the Biggleswade area. This acquisition is mentioned here as one of Atkinson's services operated into the Luton area. A Monday, Saturday and Sunday service ran between Biggleswade and Luton, which was incorporated into National's network as route 35.

Eastern National Omnibus Company Limited

The Eastern National Omnibus Company Limited name was first registered on 28 February 1929, with the company commencing operation from 1 January 1930. Eastern National had two distinct operating areas, the more traditional area of Essex, and the 'Midland Area' which covered Bedfordshire, north Buckinghamshire and east Cambridgeshire. Over a twenty-two-year period, the company operated from garages in Bedford, Luton, Biggleswade, Toddington, Hitchin, Leighton Buzzard, St Ives and Huntingdon.

The National Omnibus and Transport Company had established a garage in Castle Street, Luton in 1927, and shared this site with London General. A second garage was also in use by the company, located in Langley Street, Luton. This was acquired along with the operations of Road Motors Limited in 1925.

May 1931 saw the opening of Whipsnade Zoo, located on the edge of the Chiltern Hills on the Dunstable Downs. The new attraction brought with it competition from bus and coach operators. A number of services were established coming in from Hertfordshire and London, which will be explored further in the London Links section. A new route from Luton (LMS) station was introduced by Eastern National, numbered 53B. A second service running from Leighton Buzzard was introduced as service 67. This latter route was unsuccessful and was subsequently withdrawn. The Bedford to Dunstable service 3 was extended beyond Dunstable town centre to Whipsnade.

1930/31 saw the introduction of combined road/rail tickets on Eastern National services in the Bedford and Cambridge areas. The idea of this led to the extension of a number of services in Leighton Buzzard and Dunstable from their former town centre termini to the local railway stations. October 1931 saw the introduction of a new service linking Luton (LMS) Station-Dunstable-Fenny Stratford and Bletchley, which was numbered 66. Service 18A was extended in 1931 from Edlesborough to Leighton Buzzard, linking the two with Luton. At the same time, an express service commenced between Luton and Moggerhanger Sanatorium. November 1931 saw route 3a (Dunstable-Toddington) revert to a daily service.

A number of service changes took place in the Luton and Dunstable areas during 1932. Firstly, service 3a was revised to run between Dunstable, Charlton and Toddington, with the Tebworth journeys becoming the 3B. Service 52 (Luton-Hitchin-Letchworth-Norton-Baldock or Stotfold) was split into two, with the Luton to Baldock service retaining route number 52; the Luton to Stotfold journeys becoming service 52A. The Hockcliffe journeys on service 18 (Luton-Leighton Buzzard) retained number 18, whilst those that diverted via Tilsworth became service 18A.

By the late 1920s, the tracks of the Luton Corporation Tramway were in need of replacement. It was the prospect of replacing the track that led Luton Borough Council to enter talks with Eastern National with the view that the latter concern would purchase the network. In the first part of 1931, Eastern National put forward an offer of £64,000 for the network, which in principle was accepted by the Borough Council.

This led Eastern National to order ten Leyland Titan double-decks for tram replacement. By September 1931, the legality of the purchase was put into question, leading to its cancellation. No more came of this, and Luton Corporation later replaced the tram network with their own buses, placing applications for several services. Some of these exceeded the Borough lines of Luton, to which Eastern National and London Transport both objected.

Two routes were transferred from the United Counties Omnibus Company to Eastern National on 1 December 1933, both of which originated with the Aylesbury Motor Bus Company. The latter concern was established in 1920 by E.W. Young. During the 1920s, the Aylesbury Motor Bus Company built up a network of services covering the local area. By 1931, they had services reaching Thame, Bicester, Buckingham, Fenny Stratford, Leighton Buzzard, Dunstable, Berkhamstead, Amersham and High Wycombe. The Aylesbury company came to the attention of the Tilling Group, owners of Eastern National, in March 1933, when they made an application to the Traffic Commissioner to operate a service from Aylesbury to Northampton. This was met with objections from both Eastern National and United Counties. It was at this time that the Tilling Group made the decision to purchase the Aylesbury Motor Omnibus Company. The services were divided between various operators. Those entering Oxfordshire passed to the City of Oxford Motors, who took four routes in total on 3 August 1933. Other routes passed to Amersham and District, Thames Valley Traction Company Limited and the London Transport Passenger Board, all being transferred by December 1933. The remaining routes were split between United Counties and Eastern National. United Counties became responsible for the routes centred on Stony Stratford and Leighton Buzzard. The Aylesbury area services passed to Eastern National, two of which entered the area under review in this book. Service 2 ran between Aylesbury, Tring and Dunstable; service 3 between Berkhamstead, Tring and Dunstable. Naturally, these two services passed to Eastern National on 1 December 1933, and were renumbered 101 and 102 at this time.

Enfield based Beaumont-Safeway introduced a new service, operating into the Luton and Dunstable area in the 1930s. This company was an amalgamation of W.D. Beaumont and Safeway Saloon Coaches, set up by Arthur Priest in March 1931 who established a coach route between London, Dunstable and Leighton Buzzard, further details of which can be found in the London Links section of this book. The reason for a mention in the Eastern National section is that, in 1933 the Dunstable to Leighton Buzzard section of the service transferred to Eastern National, who incorporated it into service 18 (Luton-Dunstable-Leighton Buzzard).

1933 saw the introduction of Luton Corporation to bus operation, along with the formation of the London Transport Passenger Board. This led to the reshuffling of a number of services both within and outside of the Borough of Luton, involving these two operators and Eastern National. Further complication of the matter was made when the operations of A.F. England were acquired by Luton Corporation on 23 March 1933. This purchase, covered in further detail in the Luton Corporation section of this book, included services formerly operated by XL Services, Blue Bird and Union Jack. Luton Corporation's main interest were the routes operated under the Blue Bird name, these being local services within Luton Borough. However, England refused to sell just these, insisting that the sale must include all three operations. A number of services left the Borough boundaries, with Eastern National opposing the idea that Luton Corporation should operate these. Both operators entered talks, and an agreement was reached on 1 December 1932, known as the 'Midnight Deal'.

On this date, a reshuffle of services in the Luton and Dunstable area took place. The former Blue Bird service between Luton, Hexton and Pegsdon transferred from Luton Corporation to Eastern National, becoming service 12A. Existing service 16 was extended to Tring from Edlesborough, incorporating some of the former Aylesbury Motor Bus Company timings, along with some acquired from Luton Corporation. The frequency on services 18/18B were increased, along with an extension of the service to Wing and Burcott, incorporating former Union Jack and XL times that were transferred from Luton Corporation. Eastern National lost routes 19 (Luton-Houghton Regis-Dunstable) and 58 (Luton-Leagrave-Houghton Regis), these passing to Luton Corporation. Service 56 (Limbury-Luton Vauxhall Works) also became an all-day service.

Eastern National eradicated the last of the major competition in the Luton and Dunstable area in 1933 when, on the 23 March, the Company acquired the operations of the Bright Brothers, who traded as Bright's Luxury Coaches. With this, Eastern National gained a garage at The Square, Dunstable. Bright's was established in 1927, at which time they purchased a solitary Reo coach for use on private hire and excursion work. Further Reo saloons were soon acquired, allowing the company to commence a service between Dunstable and Edlesborough. Bright soon acquired the market day service between Leighton Buzzard and Ivinghoe, formerly operated by J.H. Pope (Reliance). Upon acquisition, the Dunstable to Edlesborough service was merged into Eastern National's existing service 16, whilst the market day service to Leighton Buzzard became service 16A. 1933 also saw the introduction of a new service, numbered 52A. It ran from Luton to Stopsley and Lilley.

A brief mention needs to be included of the operations of H.E. Hill, who traded as Strawhatter Coaches. Hill established an express service to London in 1928. After the formation of the London Passenger Transport Board in July 1933, the latter company sought to acquire this successful express service. The initial offer was rejected by H.E. Hill, but in February 1934 London Transport made a compulsory purchase of the Strawhatter operation, more details of which can be found under the London Links section. Strawhatter also operated a number of summer coastal services which immediately passed to the control of Eastern National along with eight Gilford coaches. The services ran to Southsea, Bournemouth, Margate and Great Yarmouth, with pick up points in Harpenden, Watford and St Albans.

1935 saw two new services introduced by Eastern National. The first ran between Luton and Dunstable, Hambling Place, which offered new facilities within Dunstable. It was introduced on 31 October 1935. Following in November was service 20D (Luton-Ampthill-Clophill). This was a Sunday only variation of route 20B.

The growing service portfolio and expanding fleet of vehicles saw the garage facility at Castle Street in much need of expansion. The work took place during 1936 when facilities were upgraded.

The Second World War had little effect on the operational side of Eastern National in the Luton and Dunstable area. With the exception of the coastal excursions, only one service in the Luton area was suspended. This was route 35 which ran between the town and Biggleswade. The majority of service withdrawals affected the Eastern area of the company rather than the Midland area.

In terms of damage caused to vehicles during the Second World War, the Midland area of Eastern National, unlike Luton Corporation, also fared reasonably well. Just one vehicle fell victim to the war effort. Leyland Titan 3660 (ENO938) was operating a service between Luton to Hitchin when it pulled up behind a lorry that was on fire.

The lorry was transporting bombs, and shortly after 3660 arrived on the scene, the lorry exploded, killing three passengers and injuring a number more.

The post-war housing boom created a greater need for new transport links in towns and cities around the country, linking the new housing estates. Luton and Dunstable were no exception to this. This gave rise to the expansion of the Eastern National network in the area. The first developments took place in 1947 when several routes were extended to cope with demand, operating alongside a handful of newly introduced services. Service 52D (Luton-Stopsley) was extended to serve Rochester Avenue, whilst route 57 (Luton-Leagrave) was extended to Hockwell Ring. New service 55 was introduced linking Luton with Ramridge End and Stopsley. The final service change for 1947 was the extension of service 63 (Luton-Dallow Road) out to Warren Road. The summer of 1948 saw the restoration of the coastal services to its pre-war state.

By the end of the 1940s, the housing boom in the Luton and Dunstable areas was causing both Eastern National and Luton Corporation great difficulties in attempting to extend and alter existing services to provide a transport link for these estates. The two companies were submitting a number of competing applications to the Traffic Commissioner to provide services for these new areas. It was suggested that the two concerns should come to an amicable arrangement to save time in the traffic court and to benefit themselves and passengers alike. Talks commenced between the two operators, and on 11 October 1948, an agreement was reached, known as 'Luton & District Transport'. This new initiative commenced on 1 January 1949. This saw a number of services joined, creating cross-town services. This also reduced the number of terminating points across the town. Service 55 (Park Square-Crawley Road-Stopsley) was merged with Luton Corporation's service 4 (Park Square-Dunstable Road) to form new service 4 (Dunstable Road-Park Square-Stopsley). Service 63 (Alma Street-Warren Road) was merged with Luton Corporation's service 10/11 (Library-Round Green [10]-Stopsley [11]) to form new service 11/11A, running between Warren Road, Bridge Street and Stopsley. Service 57 (LMR Station-Leagrave) was joined with service 13 (Library-Biscot Road-Leagrave) to run along the line of service 57, retaining this number. Eastern National's service between Cutenhoe Road/Vauxhall and Limbury were identified by route numbers 56/56A. They were combined with Luton Corporation's service 14 (Bridge Street-Biscot Road-Biscot Mill) to form new route 56 between Park Square and Limbury. Eastern National's service 52D (Park Square-Hart Lane-Stopsley) merged with Luton Corporation services 21 (Stopsley-Vauxhall Works-Airport [peak times only]) and 22 (Park Square-Selborne Road-Dunstable Road) to form the new service 52D (Dunstable Road-Hart Lane-Round/or Airport). Luton Corporation's service 16 (Bridge Street-Bramingham Lane) was transferred to the control of Eastern National, who renumbered it to the 14A.

Eastern National also operated numerous country services that came into the area involved in the agreement. These services were the 3 (Whipsnade Zoo-Dunstable-Toddington-Bedford); 3B (Dunstable-Tebworth-Toddington); 12 (Luton-Streatley-Shefford); 12A (Luton-Streatley-Pegsdon); 16 (Luton-Dunstable-Aylesbury); 18 (Luton-Dunstable-Leighton Buzzard); 20/A (Luton-Streatley-Bedford); 52/B (Luton-Great Offley-Baldock/Stotfold); 53 (Luton-Leagrave-Dunstable); 53A (Luton-Dunstable [direct]); 53B (Luton-Dunstable-Whipsnade Zoo); 53C (Luton-Dunstable-Hambling Place) and the 66 (Luton-Dunstable-Bletchley).

From 1 January 1948, the British Transport Commission (BTC) took control of the major railway companies in the country, along with the London Transport Passenger

Board. In September, the Tilling Group sold its bus interests to the Commission, placing Eastern National, among others, under the control of this new company. In 1952, BTC made the decision to transfer control of the 'Midland' area operations of Eastern National from Chelmsford to Northampton, placing the area under the control of the United Counties Omnibus Company Limited. The transfer took effect from May 1952. The development of services in the Luton and Dunstable area under this new owner is listed in the next sub-section.

The ECW bodied Bristol K5G formed the typical Tilling Group double-deck order for the late 1930s. 3753 (GNO697) is a fine example of the type. It was delivered to Eastern National in August 1938. *S.J. Butler Collection*

The Bristol/ECW combination was very typical of vehicles ordered by the Tilling Group. Showing off this combination is ECW bodied Bristol L5G GPU430. It was delivered to Eastern National in October 1938, taking up rolling stock number 3778. *S.J. Butler Collection*

881 (TNO674) is an ECW bodied Bristol KSW5G. Nine such vehicles were included in the Midland area transfer from Eastern National to United Counties in May 1952. 881 operated from Luton for the majority of its working life. It is photographed on Waller Street, Luton whilst operating with its new owner, United Counties. *Graham Smith*

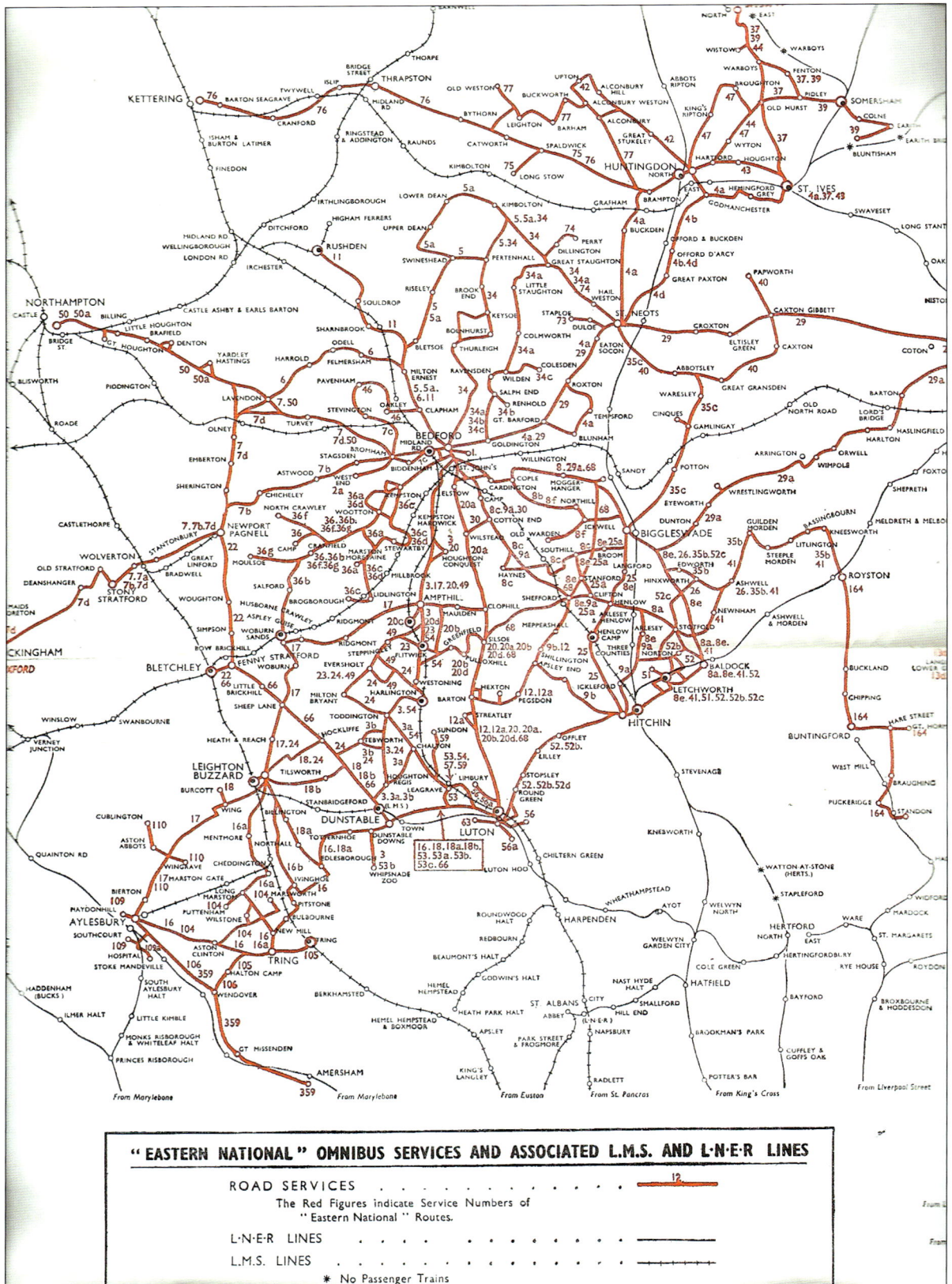

A map showing the Eastern National Midland operating area in 1949.

Until 1964, streets in the town centre were used as terminating points for Luton's bus services. The town gained its first bus station in 1964, located on land off Guildford Street, bordered by Williamson Street, Library Road and Bridge Street. The new facility was opened in August and was used by both United Counties and Luton Corporation. This was Luton's first temporary bus station.

A new service was introduced under the Luton & District Transport agreement in October 1967. The service was numbered 21 and ran between Toddington and Dunstable, via Charlton and Houghton Regis on a Monday to Friday basis. However, the service did not prove a success and was subsequently withdrawn. Just over a year later, in December 1968, service 57 was rerouted to serve the Marsh Farm housing estate.

The name Birch Bros. Limited will appear several times in this book. On 12 October 1968 Birch took the decision to give up their rural bus operations. One passed to London Transport, whilst United Counties took over the others. One of these entered the Luton area, this being the 212 between Henlow Camp and Luton, via Shillington and Barton-le-Clay. From this, three new services were introduced. The 146 took over the Luton to Henlow Camp route, running via Shillington, Campton and Meppershall. The 147 ran between the two locations, serving Shillington and Meppershall. The final service, the 148, also ran between Luton and Henlow Camp. This route served Shillington.

Five years after it opened, the first temporary bus station was closed, when on 10 August 1969, a second facility was opened on land between Williamson Street and Bridge Street. The introduction of this new facility led to withdrawn Bristol LS5G 476 (WVX441) being used by United Counties as a staff rest room, whilst withdrawn Bristol KSW5G 859 (CNH698) became a waiting room for passengers. 859 was used in this role until July 1973, when it was replaced by a temporary building.

Another significant acquisition made by United Counties was completed on 4 January 1970, when the operations of Luton Corporation Transport were purchased. An offer of £294,480 was placed by United Counties in October 1969 which was accepted. On the aforementioned date, seventy-seven buses were added to the United Counties fleet. A temporary lease of the Kingsway garage was undertaken by United Counties. The following services were inherited from Luton Corporation:

3	*Dunstable-Toddington*
6	*Luton-Houghton Regis-Dunstable*
11	*Warren Road-Wandon Close*
12	*Hockwell Ring-Round Green*
13	*Biscot Mill-Vauxhall Works*
14	*Luton-Brammington Lane*
15	*Farley Hill Estate-Vauxhall Works*
17	*Richmond Hill-Vauxhall Works*
24	*Cutenhoe Road-Vauxhall Works*
25-7	*Fountains Road-Cutenhoe Road-Hockwell Ring*
28	*Round Green-Farley Hill Estate*
29-31	*Limbury-Airport-Preistleys*
41	*Luton-Leagrave-Dunstable*
42	*Luton-Dunstable (direct)*
43	*Luton-Whipsnade Zoo*

45	*Crowland Road-Katherine Drive*
46	*Katherine Drive-Croft Estate*
50-2	*Luton-Sundon Park-Sundon*
53-4	*Luton-Toddington*
55-6	*Luton-Limbury Meads or Runfold*
57	*Luton-Leagrave-Marsh Farm*
58	*Luton-Lewsey Farm*
94/98	*Luton-Great Offley*

21 June 1970 saw the Luton and Dunstable network revised, with a number of changes made to services. The Cutenhoe Road to Town Centre section of services 25 and 27 were replaced by new services 1 and 2, with the route being extended to Stopsley.

New route 4 (Warren Road-Town Centre-Preistleys) replaced the appropriate section of routes 11, 29 and 30. Route 12 was replaced by two new routes, the 7 (Leagrave-Round Green) and the 8 (Leagrave-Regent Street). The remainder of the 29-31 group of services were replaced by routes 30 and 31. These ran from Limbury via either Fountains Road or Kingsdown Avenue to Luton Airport. These revisions led to the withdrawal of the original routes 11, 12, 25-7 and 29-31. Routes 41 and 46 were also withdrawn, being replaced by new services 58 and 59 (Luton-Leagrave-Dunstable).

Further service revisions took place during 1971 when services 94 and 98 were renumbered 62 and 63. A new service was introduced connecting the Electrolux Works to AC Delco works, travelling through Lewsey Farm and Tithe Farm Estates, which was given number 5. Service 15 was split into three new services, the 18, 19 and 20, depending on the journey it took. This trio of services also incorporated service 24, this being withdrawn. Service 57 was increased, with a circular route being added around the Marsh Farm estate. Service 144 (Luton-Pegsdon) was incorporated into the 146 to 148 group of services.

The Luton area escaped further changes until August 1973, when new service 17 was introduced to run between Park Square and Luton Airport. The Limbury to Luton Airport journeys on service 32 were transferred across to the 31. A second new service to be introduced was the 33, operating between Luton Bus Station and Wigmore Lane Estate.

Independent operator Court Line Coaches went into receivership in August 1974 but continued to operate for a further four months. After negotiations between United Counties, Bedfordshire and Hertfordshire County Councils and Luton Airport Management, the company took over seven services focused on the Dunstable and Hemel Hempstead areas. Since the routes taken over from Court Line entered the 'Metropolitan' area to the south of Luton, the acquisition of Court Line by United Counties is covered in greater detail in the following section.

United Counties took the decision in February 1975 to revise some of its services in the Luton and Dunstable area to help improve their reliability. Services 1 and 2 (Cutenhoe Road-Luton town centre-Stopsley) were incorporated into new services 5 and 25, taking the Stopsley to town centre section. The Cutenhoe Road to Luton town centre section of the services were merged into services 11 and 12 (via London Road) and 9 and 10 (via Park Street). The former service 5 (Electrolux Works to A C Delco Works) was renumbered 39. Service 6 (Luton-Houghton Regis-Dunstable) was also renumbered, becoming the 36, becoming one-person-operated. Services 7 and 8 (Round Green-Hockwell Ring), 9 (Vauxhall Works-Hockwell Ring) and 10 (SKF Works to Electrolux Works) were altered and covered by several new services. The route between Round Green and Luton town centre became services 7 and 8; the Hockwell Ring-Selbourne Road-town centre service was numbered 5. Service 25 took over the section of route between Hockwell Ring, Leagrave Road and Luton town centre. Service 10 was split, being renumbered to the 15 and 53. Service 33 was extended from Wigmore Lane to Dunstable.

At the same time, service 23 (Dunstable-Sundon SKF Works) was renumbered to the 13, with a reduction in journeys. Routes 30 and 31 (Luton Airport-town centre-Icknield Road) were replaced by a number of new services. The 30, 31 and 32 continued to operate journeys between Luton and Luton Airport. This trio of services were extended to operate to Dunstable, replacing service 42. Services 7 and 8 took over the section of route running from the town centre to Bancroft Road and Trinity Road, with service 8 continuing on to terminate at Neville Road. A small section of the former 30 and 31 routes between the town centre and Badgers Hill was incorporated in service 26. Service 33 (Wigmore Lane Estate-Luton Bus Station) was replaced by a new service, also numbered 33, which continued its journey on through to Dunstable. Routes 44 and 45 (Stopsley-Wheatfield Road (44) and Katherine Drive (45)) were also replaced. Service 44 became service 38, whilst the Katherine Drive section of service 45 was incorporated into the new route 33 mentioned above. Services 55 and 56 (Town Centre-Biscot Mill-Limbury Meads-Runfold) were replaced by six services. New routes 8, 10 and 12 ran between Luton town centre and Limbury, whilst the 7, 9 and 11 operated between Luton town centre and Runfold. The reshaping of Luton's services at this time saw the London overspill estate at Tithe Farm gain a good service from United Counties. The former Court Line services were also renumbered by the company, and as with the takeover, details of this renumbering can be found in the following chapter.

The acquisition of the Luton Corporation fleet in 1970, placed a strain on the garaging facilities at Castle Street. Funding for an extension and the construction of new facilities were approved, and work commenced in 1973. Included in these plans were five additional maintenance pits, a new administrative block incorporating offices, a staff canteen and leisure facilities. The improvements were met with delays, opening in September 1975.

In the summer of 1975, independent operator Jey-Son Coaches announced that they wished to withdraw their bus service commitments. In July of this year, the Luton-Breachwood Green-Hitchin service passed to the control of United Counties, originally being numbered as the 81. The service was renumbered 88 in 1976 when control of the service transferred from Luton to Hitchin. The other Jey-Son service passed to fellow National Bus Company subsidiary London Country. However, in 1976 United Counties was approached by Bedfordshire County Council with a request to take over the operation of two services running south of the town from London Country Bus Services. The services concerned were service 360 (Luton-Caddington) and service 365 (Luton-Kimpton-Codicote). The Luton to Caddington service was soon incorporated into the Luton town service network, as service 6. It was soon extended from Luton Bus Station to Warden Hill Road replacing service 26, being converted to one-man operation at the same time. Service 365 was also renumbered, this time to service 45. The Friday and Saturday service on this route was soon replaced by a new Monday to Saturday service 44, running between Luton and Stevenage, running via Kimpton and Codicote. This new service was jointly operated with London Country Bus Services from Stevenage for a short period of time. The 44 commenced operation on 1 October 1977.

Unfortunately, service economies soon proved necessary on the United Counties' network of country services. The Dunstable-Hemel Hempstead service 41 was merged with the long-established Luton-Dunstable-Whipsnade Zoo service 43 to operate under the latter service number. It ran between Luton and Hemel Hempstead via Dunstable, Kensworth, Whipsnade Zoo, Studham and Gaddesden Row, also replacing former services 42 between Luton and Whipsnade via Markyate, and the 47 between Luton and Hemel Hempstead. Service 46 (Luton-Flamstead-M1-Hemel Hempstead) was diverted off the motorway, to serve Redbourn, this in turn allowing London Country to reduce their service 307. The daytime frequency on service 40 (Luton-Slip End-Woodside-Aley Green-Caddington-Dunstable) was severely reduced, and merged with service 63 (Bedford-Dunstable) to provide a roundabout route between Luton and Bedford, via Dunstable. The service was typically operated by one-man-operated Bristol VRTs. However, the 63 did not operate in the evenings. To compensate for this, new service 41 was introduced, operating in a circular style between Luton, Slip End, Woodsie, Aley Green, Caddington and Luton. A Sunday service on the route was also introduced after the withdrawal of service 6. The former service 44 between Dunstable and Dagnall was replaced for a while by the extension of some Luton-Edlesborough short workings on service 61 (Luton-Aylesbury), running from Edlesborough Village via the Traveller's Rest to Dagnall. This was again a long-winded service, and it is thought because of this that it killed off any passenger demand.

A third bus station was constructed in Luton, opening for business on 5 September 1976. A new undercover facility was constructed in Bute Street, adjacent to the town's Midland railway station. London Country and National Express began using the station from this date, with United Counties following suit a week later. The former, temporary, bus station remained in use for a short while whilst other infrastructure was built in the surrounding streets, and to allow for demolition work to take place in nearby Manchester Street.

Further service changes took place on 17 July 1977 when services 7 to 12 were renumbered 8 to 11 and converted to one-person-operation. Route 8 operated between Limbury Meads and Luton town centre; route 9 between Cutenhoe Road, Luton town centre and Runfold; the 10 between Luton town centre and Limbury Meads. Service 11 linked Runfold with Luton town centre and Round Green, this latter route replacing parts of former routes 7 and 8.

Four buses were destroyed and five others damaged after arsonists struck at Luton garage on 25 February 1979. The majority of vehicles affected were ECW bodied Bristol RELL6Ls, with a pair of Leyland National saloons also falling victim. Services 5 and 25 were also converted to one-person-operation at this time, being extended from Wigmore Lane Estate to Telscombe Way and Selsey Drive.

Two London overspill estates had been built during the 1970s near to Houghton Regis, named Lewsey Farm and Tithe Farm. United Counties served these two estates with service 36. The route involved a turn off the main road, and a turn-around at Dolphin Drive, before the service returned back to the main road and continued its journey to Houghton Regis and Dunstable. A third overspill estate was planned in between the two existing estates, to be named Parkside. To help United Counties with the operational side of service 36, the company approached Bedfordshire County Council about constructing a 'buslink' between the two estates, giving a more direct link to the three areas. The County Council was keen on this idea, but opposition was met from Luton Borough and South Bedfordshire Councils. However, these oppositions were not upheld by the County Council, and on 4 November 1979, a half-mile single-track buslink was opened through the Parkside estate, with the United Counties network of services in that area being revised at the same time. Service 39 was renumbered 33 and ran between Dunstable A C Delco Works-Tithe Farm-Parkside-Buslink-Lewsey Farm-Leagrave Electrolux Works; service 35 ran between Dunstable, Southwood Road, Tithe Farm, Parkside, Bus Link and Luton Bus Station. Service 37 (Dunstable, Southwood Road to Luton Bus Station) was diverted to run via Tithe Farm and Parkside. Service 38 was revised to run between Lewsey

A map showing the route taken by the new Buslink through the Parkside Estate. *Roger Warwick Collection*

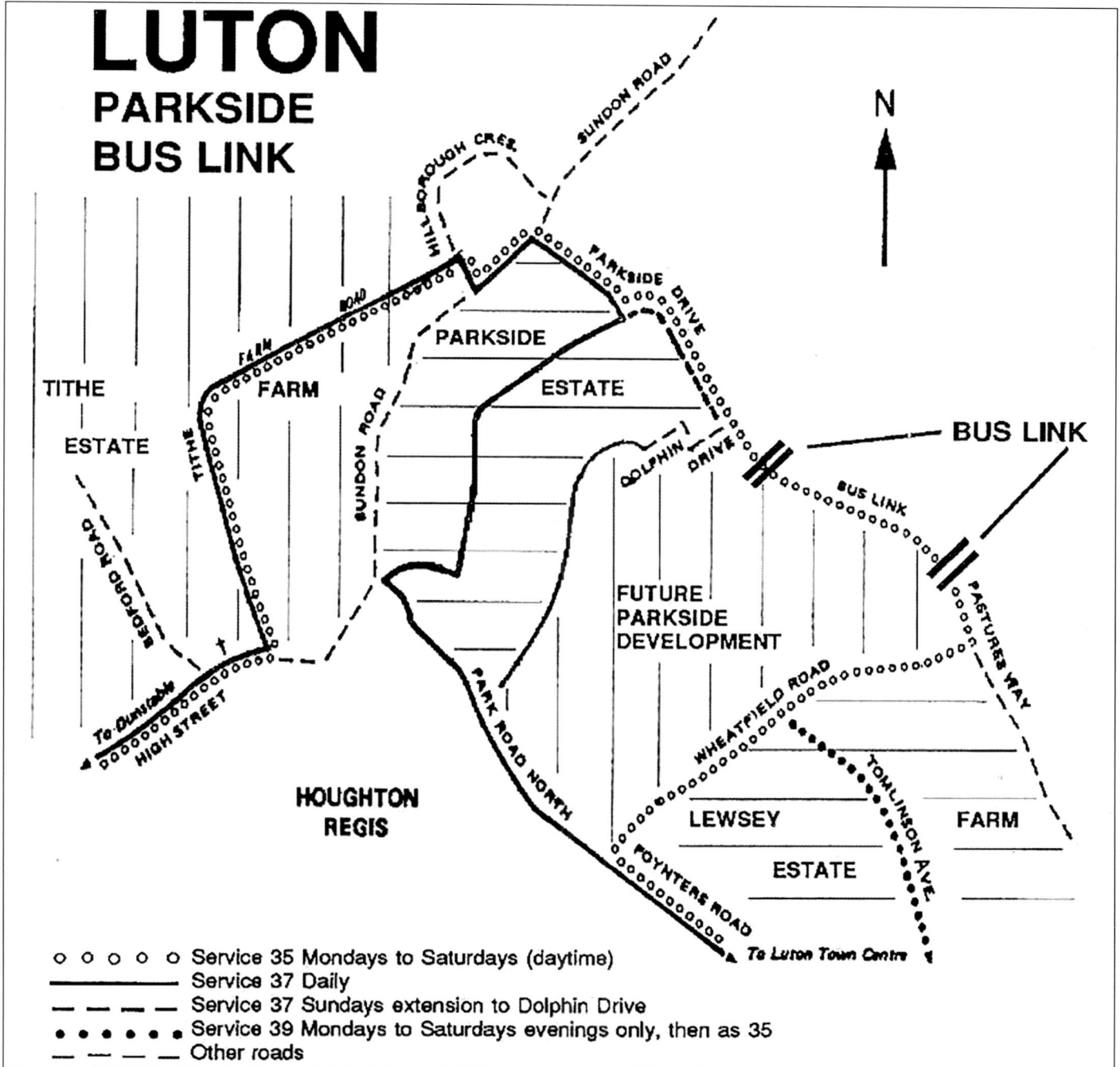

LUTON
PARKSIDE
BUS LINK

N

TITHE ESTATE

PARKSIDE ESTATE

BUS LINK

FUTURE PARKSIDE DEVELOPMENT

HOUGHTON REGIS

LEWSEY ESTATE

FARM

To Luton Town Centre

o o o o o Service 35 Mondays to Saturdays (daytime)
——— Service 37 Daily
— — — — Service 37 Sundays extension to Dolphin Drive
• • • • • Service 39 Mondays to Saturdays evenings only, then as 35
— · — · — Other roads

Farm, Luton and Stopsley. Finally, a new service 39 was introduced and ran between Dunstable, Southwood Road and Stopsley, via Tithe Farm, Parkside, Buslink, Lewsey Farm and Luton town centre.

A new route 7 was also introduced to link George Street and Ashton Road during 1979 to appease residents who were not happy at withdrawals previously made by United Counties from this area.

Furthermore, minor service changes took place during 1980, affecting services 9, 11, 23 and 24. Service 9 was diverted away from Cutenhoe Road, but gained the Park Square to Runfold section of route 11. Country area services 23 and 24 (Luton-Flitwick-Ampthill) lost the section of route between Flitwick and Ampthill.

As was mentioned in the introduction, over the years Luton has been home to many independent operators. One such operator was a small minibus company called Lunar Module. A number of applications to the Traffic Commissioner were made by this company during the early 1980s. In 1982, Lunar Module was again refused an operators' licence, leading to the company lodging a complaint with the Minister of Transport. A decision was made by the Minister in July 1983, granting the company a licence. Lunar Module commenced operation in Luton on 3 May 1984 and it was between this date and December 1985 that the company became a significant competitor for United Counties and later Luton & District. In July 1988, Lunar Module became known as Lutonian. To prepare for the arrival of Lunar Module, United Counties increased publicity both at bus stops and on their buses. The company also introduced a central fare zone for 15p.

The National Bus Company took the decision to split its operating companies up into smaller units over the course of 1985, to make it easier to sell them, with United Counties being no exception. The company was therefore split into four operating companies, with effect from 1 January 1986. United Counties retained its garages at Bedford, Biggleswade, Corby, Huntingdon, Kettering, Northampton and Wellingborough. Milton Keynes became its own company, known as Milton Keynes Citybus. The third, and final, bus operation became Luton & District. This new company took on responsibility for garages at Aylesbury, Dunstable, Hitchin and Luton. The fourth company formed was known as United Counties Engineering.

The division of United Counties did not spell the end of the company's presence in the Luton and Dunstable areas. A new express coach network was introduced on 25 May 1986, branded 'Coachlinks'. The initial Coachlinks network was centred on Bedford, with two services also serving Luton. The first was the X1 which ran from Peterborough, via Huntingdon, St Neots and Bedford, before continuing to Luton and Luton Airport. In October, the X1 was extended southwards to Heathrow Airport, Slough and Windsor, lasting until July 1987 when the Heathrow to Windsor section was withdrawn. The second service was numbered X2, and linked Luton and Luton Airport with Bedford and Northampton, serving the villages between the latter two towns.

United Counties felt threatened by the encroachment of Luton & District close to the small Bedfordshire town of Flitwick, a town which had been a strong hold of United Counties and its predecessors. Therefore, United Counties set up another Coachlinks service in the Luton & District operating area as a warning to them. The service took up number X6, and ran between Husborne Crawley and Luton, via Leighton Buzzard and Dunstable.

In November 1987, United Counties was acquired by Stagecoach Holdings Ltd, Perth. This eventually brought about the white based livery, relieved by orange, red and blue stripes.

April 1990 saw United Counties acquire a pair of school contracts that ran into the Luton area after the collapse of Kempston based Horseshoe Coaches. Service 915 ran from the Luton estates direct to Bedford High School, whilst service 916 ran from Luton to Bedford High School, serving the villages on the way.

Over the coming years, very little changed in the Luton area in terms of United Counties. One event to note was the diversion of 'Coachlinks' service X52 (Corby-Kettering-Rushden-Bedford-London) to serve Luton. The London terminus of this service was at Marylebone Station. The introduction of European driving hours to coach services in the UK in 1998 affected the through journeys operating on United Counties' Coachlinks services. By the end of the year, the X2 was curtailed between Northampton and Bedford, no longer operating between Bedford and Luton. The X1 continued to operate between Bedford and Luton, the Heathrow Airport provision being withdrawn.

United Counties was successful in winning another service in the Luton area in 1999. The contract for a rail link between Luton Airport, Luton and Milton Keynes was won, operating under the 'Virgin Rail Link' brand, numbered VT99. The Stagecoach Group owned a 49 per cent share in Virgin Trains. To operate this service, three coaches were acquired and allocated to nearby Bedford. The intention of this service was to provide a direct and easy link between the West Coast Main Line and Midland main line railways, as well as Luton Airport itself. The route also provided Luton with a link to the Stagecoach Express X5 service between Cambridge and Oxford. A fourth coach was added to the service in 2000. The fleet was renewed in 2003, bringing with it a revised livery. The first wheelchair accessible coaches operated by United Counties were allocated to the VT99 in 2006. The Virgin Rail Link element of the service was later terminated, and the VT99 continued to operate along the same route on a commercial basis, taking service number 99. An assortment of vehicles was used on the service, with the accessible coaches initially operating the service. In 2015, the X5 service was restocked with new coaches, leading to a handful of the former X5 coaches being re-allocated to the 99 service. A small number of these gained route branding.

During 2013, Bedford garage transferred to sister Stagecoach company Cambus Limited, based in Cambridge. United Counties itself ceased to exist in October 2014, when the Northamptonshire operations were merged with Stagecoach Warwickshire, to form the new Stagecoach Midlands group, operating on the Midland Red South operators' licence.

A number of service changes took place in the Luton area on 23 July 2000 affecting services operated by Arriva the Shires that left the Luton area and entered Central Bedfordshire. From this date two of these services, the 78 and 79 between Luton, Barton and Henlow, were withdrawn by Arriva and re-awarded to Stagecoach United Counties, running on Mondays to Saturdays.

United Counties relaunched the country area services operated from Bedford, using the names of planets, this also leading to the renumbering of services. Two of the services entered the Luton and Dunstable area. The Luton service was branded *Saturn*, gaining new route number S1. A trio of Northern Counties bodied Volvo Olympians were branded for the service. The Bedford to Dunstable service was branded as *Jupiter* and numbered J1, these also being operated by Northern Counties bodied Volvo Olympians.

Stagecoach East made a number of service cuts in Bedfordshire on 18 February 2007. These included the withdrawal of the 78 and 79 services mentioned above. At this time, Centrebus took over the 79, and extended it out to Meppershall, replacing the 78 which was completely withdrawn. From this date, the J1 service was curtailed to operate between Bedford and Flitwick, losing its Flitwick to Dunstable provision, the latter being taken over by Grant Palmer of Dunstable.

Stagecoach withdrew its Planet network from 21 August 2011. From this date, the S1 Saturn service became the 81, and continued to operate along the same route as before.

As of December 2020, Stagecoach continues to operate two services into Luton under the Cambus Limited operation. These are the 81 (Bedford-Elstow-Wixhams-Clophill-Silsoe-Barton-le-Clay-Luton) and the 99 (Milton Keynes-Luton-Luton Airport), both continuing to operate from Bedford depot.

In 1969 United Counties staff at Luton garage were preparing for the acquisition of Luton Corporation Transport at the end of the year. This led to a shortage of serviceable buses at Luton. To help out, Bedford sent Bristol K5G 831 (FRP685) to Luton. It is seen on a wet December day, departing Mill Street, Luton on service 55 to Limbury Mead Estate. 831 was withdrawn in January 1970, with its fleet number being reallocated to an Albion Lowlander inherited from Luton Corporation. *Graham Smith*

ECW bodied
Bristol KSW6B 864 (CNH703) formed part of an order of twenty such vehicles allocated to United Counties in 1952. 864 was allocated to Luton where it remained for the duration of its working life, until it was withdrawn in June 1970. It is seen in Beachwood Road, heading towards the Roman Road terminus of service 12.
Graham Smith

897 (CNH717) is another example of the twenty Bristol KSW6Bs delivered to the company during 1952. This is one of six that entered service the day of the transfer of Eastern National's Midland area to United Counties in May 1952. 897 was another KSW6B to have remained at Luton for its working life. It is seen at the Sundon 'Red Lion' terminus, whilst operating service 52.
Graham Smith

ECW bodied Bristol KSW6B 944 (JBD981) is seen departing the Hockwell Ring terminus, travelling along Mayne Avenue whilst operating service 12 to Round Green in November 1969. 944 formed part of a batch of eighteen KSW6Bs delivered to United Counties during 1953. Like the other three Bristol double-deckers featured above, 944 also operated for the majority of its career with United Counties from Luton garage. *Graham Smith*

A number of buses operated by United Counties between 1960 and 1980 are covered in the Luton Corporation and Luton & District sections of this book. We fast forward to the 1980s, when United Counties upgraded their coaching fleet using a number of Leyland Leopard and Leyland Tiger coaches. Plaxton Paramount bodied Leyland Tiger 121 (C122PNV) is seen passing through Luton whilst operating a journey on a Coachlinks service X2 to Northampton. *Gary Seamarks*

Between 1993 and 1997, United Counties took stock of sizable numbers of Plaxton Premiere bodied Volvo B10M coaches to update the 'Coachlinks' network. Kettering based 185 (R185DNH) represents the final batch of thirteen B10M coaches and is seen on layover at Luton Bute Street bus station. *Gary Seamarks*

1999 saw the introduction of a service linking Milton Keynes Station with Luton and Luton Airport. Branded under the 'Virgin Rail Link' name, three Berkhof Excellence bodied Volvo B10M coaches were acquired from Stagecoach Oxford. A fourth was added in October 2000 registered 3063VC. It is this vehicle we see below, on layover at Luton Airport showing off the original route livery. 3063VC was numbered 167 by United Counties and allocated to Bedford. *Gary Seamarks*

Above: **In October** 2006, six Plaxton Profile bodied Volvo B7R coaches were purchased by United Counties for the Virgin Rail Link service between Luton Airport, Luton and Milton Keynes. 53272 (KX56JZK) is seen wearing the third livery worn by coaches used on this service. It is seen approaching the terminus at Luton Airport. *David Beddall*

Opposite above: **July 2000** saw routes 78 and 79 pass from Arriva the Shires to United Counties. Bedford based Northern Counties bodied Leyland Olympian 14065 (K665UNH) is seen on layover at Luton Bus Station before setting off on another journey to Henlow Camp on the 78. *Nick Doolan*

Opposite below: **The upgrade** of rolling stock on the X5 (Cambridge to Oxford) service led to the upgrade of the coaching fleet used by Cambus on the 99 service. 53615 (KX58NCN) is seen departing Luton Interchange to complete the short journey to Luton Airport. Route branding of varying degrees was applied to the coaches, with full route branding being applied to 53615. *Liam Farrer-Beddall*

In 2013, Bedford garage transferred to the control of Cambus Limited. Under the new owners, the fleet at Bedford was upgraded several times with vehicles cascaded from other Cambus garages. In 2018, Stagecoach East's King's Lynn garage closed leaving a number of surplus vehicles. The opportunity was taken by Cambus to transfer a number of the newer vehicles from King's Lynn to Bedford. 37433 (SN16OPX) was one of nine AD E20D/Enviro 200 MMC saloons to have made the transfer. It is seen loading outside the Galaxy Centre in Luton town centre. *Liam Farrer-Beddall*

30 August 2020 saw the X5 service curtailed to operate between Bedford and Oxford. The Bedford to Cambridge section was renumbered 905 and operated by double-deckers from this date. This led to a number of coaches becoming surplus, and they were put to use on the 99, replacing the Volvo B9Rs. The last of the batch, 54318 (YX64WDD), is seen approaching its stop at Luton Interchange, showing off the full X5 livery. *Liam Farrer-Beddall*

CHAPTER THREE
LONDON LINKS

I t has already been mentioned in the introduction that Luton fell into two traffic areas, the Eastern and Metropolitan. The latter traffic area led to a number of London operators operating routes into the Luton and Dunstable area. It is in this section that we take a look at how the routes in this area developed.

The first motorbus operation recorded in this area commenced in August 1909 when the landlord of the Peahen Hotel, St Albans started a service between St Albans and Redbourn, trading as the Hertfordshire Motor Omnibus Company. The route was operated by a double-deck bus of an unknown type. The service was soon expanded to serve Markyate. Plans were made in 1910 to extend this service to Dunstable. Although it was heavily publicised in the local press, it does not seem to have commenced operation. It is likely that approval to ply for hire, then the responsibility of local authorities, may not have been forthcoming in Bedfordshire. The service continued for a while between St Albans and Markyate but ceased some time during 1911. In 1911, the landlord of the 'Saracen's Head' in High Street South, Dunstable, Hugh Jones, purchased two charabancs and began trading as the Dunstable Road Car Company. Under this name, Jones attempted to run a bus service between Dunstable and Luton. However, he was immediately intercepted by the Luton Borough Police and forced to curtail his operations at the Dunstable Road tram terminus, located at the present-day Dunstable Road/Kingsway junction in Luton. The level of service provided was never good, and varied from month to month, often only operating on Saturdays. He persevered briefly, under his flamboyant full name of Hugh MacKenzie Smellie Beale Jones (H.M.S. Beale Jones), relaunching his operations as the Bedfordshire Road Car Company. For this new venture, he purchased four redundant Thornycrofts from the London General Omnibus Company, two of which were fitted with double-deck bodies. The occasional service to the Luton tram terminus was supplemented by a service to Leighton Buzzard. Before the company collapsed there were proposals for a service to Markyate. At the end of 1911, the vehicles were sold to Henry Burridge of Bedford.

The northwards expansion of the London motorbus services of the London General Omnibus Company (LGOC), owned by the Underground Group from January 1912, had reached St Albans in 1912 and Watford in 1913, but only as termini for services from Greater London. At this time the LGOC were operating two services into that area, the 84 between Golders Green and St Albans and the 105 (Kilburn Park-Watford), this latter service later being renumbered 142. It is thought that at this time there were no other motorbuses running in St Albans. Watford was served by motorbuses operated by the London & North Western Railway Company (LNWR), which had been operating both local and country services since 1906. The main-line railway companies were only empowered to operate motorbuses in direct connection with their railway operations at that time. The buses had been introduced to thwart a BET proposal for an electric tramway network in Watford. The outbreak of War in 1914 somewhat changed the situation and LNWR withdrew all of its bus services from April 1915, apart from a few works journeys which lasted until 1917.

During the war, LGOC maintained services 84 and 142, before being approached by the local authorities in Watford and St Albans to set up local bus operations in the two towns. However, London General was very reluctant to get involved with local bus services in Hertfordshire but gave in and established a new garage in Leavesden Road, Watford in August 1920. At this time, a series of routes numbered in the 140s commenced, including the 143 to St Albans. Local services then commenced in St Albans, Welwyn Garden City and Hatfield where garages were also constructed. London General's services in Hertfordshire were operating at a loss, with competitors offering similar services, with cheaper running costs. To combat this, LGOC struck a deal in 1921 with the National Steam Car Company Limited. The first was for National to withdraw from Greater London, with operations transferring to London General, and the Bedfordshire operations of LGOC transferring to National. This is referred to in more detail in the National section.

The second deal was agreed with the Underground Group during the early months of 1921. It identified an area, mostly within Hertfordshire between North London and a radius of 30 miles from Charing Cross, in which buses and garages would be financed and provided by London General. National would lease these and employ staff and provide the services. The Luton-Harpenden-St Albans road was excluded from this, as Road Motors Ltd. had operated the service since January 1921; a separate deal was later agreed between London General, National and Road Motors in 1921. This resulted in Road Motors withdrawing its St Albans to Hertford service which they had commenced from an outstation in St Albans, while National gave up their Luton-Toddington and Dunstable-Leagrave services in favour of Road Motors Ltd. The rights to the Luton to St Albans, Luton to Markyate and Luton to Wheathampstead services were retained by Road Motors, although London General was allowed to extend their service 84 from St Albans to Harpenden as service 84A at weekends, which proved to be unsuccessful and was soon withdrawn.

The existing London General services at Watford, with the exception of the 142 from Kilburn Park, passed into National control, along with the new garage at Hatfield once it was completed. Although the Leavesden Road, Watford garage was used by National for a while, it was soon replaced by new premises in Watford High Street, which initially offered larger accommodation. The Leavesden Road garage remained London General property but was out of use for a number of years in the 1920s.

Mention should be made at this point of the Dunstable-Redbourn service, which had been introduced in autumn 1920 under the local Dunstable area service number 8. In June 1921, National eliminated the local area service number schemes and renumbered all services within Bedfordshire under a common numbering sequence, when it briefly became service 21. Almost immediately, the deal with London General came into effect and service 21 was extended from Redbourn to St Albans and designated as a service operated on behalf of London General, which were to be renumbered in the 200 series, becoming route 200. This service number scheme was quickly rejected, however, and replaced in August 1921 by use of 'N' prefix to the service number to indicate services to the north of London. A similar scheme made with the East Surrey Traction Company to the south of London used 'S' prefixes whilst a scheme with the Thames Valley Traction Company in 1922 to the west of London used 'W' prefixes; the latter scheme did not stand the test of time and was soon dissolved. At this point, the St Albans-Dunstable bus service became service N4, the fourth service number in three months.

Country area bus services based on the Luton area continued to develop in 1921, this being done by Road Motors Ltd, as well as smaller businesses based in Luton and surrounding villages. John Frost, Arthur Carter and Sidney Hawkins had established a motor vehicle garage in Ashburnham Road, Luton, Frost being a sleeping partner, and soon expanded into road haulage. By the end of 1921, the trio had commenced an extremely rural daily bus route between Luton and Hitchin via Spittlesea Wood, Danestreet, Breachwood Green, Kings Walden, Whitehall Farm and Preston using small capacity one-man buses, under the FCH Motor Haulage and Engineering Company title. In November 1921, Arthur William Burnage, of Chobham Street, Luton, advertised a daily bus service between Kimpton, Wheathampstead, Batford and Luton, although he had no bus to run it, hiring one from Road Motors Ltd. Soon after, Road Motors commenced their own service between Luton, Batford and Wheathampstead. After this time, Burnage hired a bus from Stormer Bros. who were based in Jubilee Street, Luton. The latter operator again established a service over a similar route. In January 1922, Stormer Bros. decided to operate the bus service themselves between Luton and Wheathampstead. Burnage made several further applications to Luton Borough Watch Committee for permission to ply for hire on the Luton Borough section of this route in the ensuing years, each being rejected as he was unable to produce a vehicle for police approval. Meanwhile, Road Motors Ltd. had also commenced a daily service to Woodside, Slip End and Markyate, in November 1921, a service which proved very popular. The Wheathampstead service, possibly affected by the parallel Great Northern Railway branch line (Hatfield-Luton-Dunstable) failed to generate significant revenue leading to Road Motors' service being reduced to two journeys on Saturdays only. Stormer Bros. withdrew from the service in June 1923, replaced by A.K. Milner, of Hightown Road, Luton, who operated a through service between Luton and St Albans via Batford and Wheathampstead, with some journeys diverting to serve Kimpton. The latter operator was slightly more successful, but still disappeared from the scene during 1924.

A number of other bus services entered the Luton and Dunstable area from the south. Carr & Hollings, who traded as Local Bus, operated into Dunstable from Berkhamsted and Hemel Hempstead mainly on a Wednesday (market day) and Saturday. West Herts Motor Services introduced a daily service from Boxmoor via Hemel Hempstead, Gaddesden, Studham and Dunstable Downs probably from 1923. The Carr & Hollings business was later merged into S.H. Viles' 'Pioneer Bus Service'. In the opposite direction, National introduced several Saturday journeys as a new service 16B, a variant of their Luton-Ivinghoe service 16 and Luton-Edlesborough service 16A, both outside the Luton and Dunstable area, operating between Dunstable, Dunstable Downs and Studham. In the following year, these journeys were extended to operate through to and from Luton.

The Luton-Harpenden-St Albans service remained exclusively operated by Road Motors Ltd., using mainly ex-War Department Dennis lorry chassis on which second-hand ex-London General B type bodies, both double-deck and cut down single-decks, were mounted. This was a low-cost way of providing buses at this time. Competition was met in late 1923 on the St Albans service, Road Motors' most profitable service, the threat coming from the Morgan Brothers, Alfred and Philip, from South East London. The former, a retired Army officer, was the dominant driving force, buying a new Lancia coach on pneumatic tyres, kept initially in a yard in Latimer Road, Luton, but later moved to premises in Harpenden, where Alfred Morgan was now lodging. With the coach body well appointed, including curtains and small vases of flowers affixed to the window frames, he offered a limited bus service between Luton, Harpenden and St Albans in competition with Road Motors' much more frequent service using former army lorries. Further Lancia coaches appeared in a vivid silver livery, prompting Road Motors to buy several pneumatic-tyred Model T Ford chassis on which 12-seat or 14-seat bus bodies were built by Waveney Coachworks of Lowestoft, with the objective of chasing Morgan's coaches to try to prevent prospective passengers from boarding them. The Fords chased, but rarely caught. Competition on the route soon ceased, with Road Motors and the Morgan Brothers, who were now trading as Comfy Coaches, agreeing a co-ordinated timetable. The Ford T types were removed by Road Motors to introduce a one-man operated town service along Dallow Road in Luton, whilst the Comfy Car fleet, which eventually comprised just 4 coaches, was housed in a large new garage and filling station built in 1930 on the corner of Townsend Lane and Harpenden High Street.

At the same time as the Morgans began operations, the Luton-St Albans service saw occasional journeys operated by one vehicle owned by Arthur Blowers, trading as Harmony, this being a second-hand Sunbeam chassis on which a new 13-seat bus body was fitted. Arthur Blowers had previously been a mechanic with Marlborough Motors in St Albans, and his bus was kept in a nearby yard in Marlborough Road. His departure times on the Luton service were subsequently co-ordinated with those operated by Comfy Cars and Road Motors, and he soon changed his name to Express. Further vehicles were acquired and other bus operations commenced on local services within St Albans, an area full of competition. In 1927, Express commenced another service between Fleetville, St Albans and Markyate, which was later extended to Dunstable. The introduction of this route overstretched Blowers' resources. He undertook the maintenance work on his vehicles which meant that upon inspection by Hertfordshire Police, a number of vehicles were declared as being unfit for use. This resulted in the Dunstable service ceasing, although the Luton service continued.

At the beginning of 1924, new country bus services entered Luton from the east of the town. The first came from Whitwell by way of Bendish and Danestreet, operated by Ansell William Bailey-Hawkins. The Bailey-Hawkins were a husband-and-wife team of entrepreneurs based at Stagenhoe Bottom Farm, to the north of St. Paul's Walden. A number of other business interests were run by the pair, including a filling station in Whitwell and a coal merchant business in Letchworth, Hitchin and Luton. A charabanc hire and bus service business was added to their portfolio in 1924. The main bus service provided was daily between Whitwell and Hitchin, but the service to Luton only normally ran on three days per week, Thursday, Saturday and Sunday. During the summer months the service was upgraded to a daily operation. One of the drivers employed was also Whitwell's village carpenter, Arthur Hancock, who was also the licence holder for one of the village's pubs! In 1925, Arthur Hancock assumed ownership of the bus and charabanc operations from the Bailey-Hawkins, buying a cottage with adjoining yard in Horn Hill, Whitwell from which the vehicles now operated under the fleet name 'Whitwell Bus Service'.

Around the same time, May 1924, Clarence William 'Bill' Jones started the Enterprise Bus Service, running between Welwyn, Kimpton, Peter's Green and Luton. His elder brother, Arthur Leonard Jones, owned the Enterprise garage in Elizabeth Street, Luton where the Enterprise bus(es) were initially based. His father, Fred Jones, was landlord of the Bright Star, located in the hamlet of Peter's Green, which was adjacent to the Bedfordshire/Hertfordshire border. The narrow lanes in the area restricted the Enterprise fleet to small capacity vehicles, with no more than 25-seaters, with one-man operation always the rule. The popularity of Peter's Green as a summer destination for people from urban Luton meant the bus business was successful. The Enterprise Garage was moved to larger premises in Bailey Street, Luton in 1927, then in 1930 to Peter's Green itself, opposite the Bright Star and alongside the Half Moon.

1924 also saw Road Motors introduce a short service between Luton and Caddington Green. At the same time, some journeys on the FCH service between Luton, Breachwood Green and Hitchin were diverted to serve the hamlet of Ley Green.

The following year commenced with the introduction of several additional country services into the area of study, namely a new Road Motors' service to Hemel Hempstead, via Batford, Harpenden and Redbourn. It is believed to have been a Saturday only operation, although no days of operation were shown on publicity. Shortly afterwards, FCH introduced journeys between Luton and Tea Green, mostly via Nether Crawley Farm and Cockernhoe, but with some journeys via Round Green, Stopsley, Ramridge End and Cockernhoe. The latter, longer route may have been considered necessary for busier journeys in view of the steepness of Crawley Green Road encountered on the normal route.

Mention has already been made of the acquisition of Road Motors by National in April 1925. A list of services operated in the Eastern Traffic area at the time of takeover can be found under the National section. However, a number of services also operated into the Metropolitan Traffic area, these being as follows: Luton-St Albans which became service 51; Luton-Markyate numbered 55; Luton-Caddington became service 60; Luton-Wheathampstead service 61 and Luton-Hemel Hempstead was numbered 66. The latter service, however, appears to have been quickly revised, if it did ever operate to Hemel Hempstead, to operate as a circular route in one direction, returning from Redbourn to Luton via Markyate, Woodside, Manor Road and Caddington, instead of running to Hemel Hempstead. In this guise, it became a Saturday only service, but was not successful and ceased entirely in 1929.

Although the ageing Palladium double-decks acquired from Road Motors were retained at Luton, the ex-War Department Dennis vehicles were largely rebodied with new single-deck bodies, some of which were fitted with pneumatic tyres and transferred to less arduous duties, often in the West Country. In Luton, AEC YC vehicles with the larger capacity (44/46 seat) double-deck bodies, sometimes rebuilt with enclosed cabs, were transferred in, although these were already over five years old.

During 1925, ownership of the FCH business in Luton passed from Frost, Carter and Hawkins to the business's manager, C.D. Thompson, who immediately indicated he wished only to retain the garage, motor engineering and road haulage part of the business, putting the buses up for sale. Following the expensive acquisition of Road Motors Ltd., there was no money in the National Omnibus & Transport Company's budget for further business acquisitions. The Underground Group provided a solution. As a result of the acquisition of Road Motors' services by National, it was being considered that the area in which vehicles and premises were provided by London General for operations by National be extended northwards to include Harpenden, the southern part of Luton and Hertfordshire as far north as the south side of the A505 Luton to Hitchin road. The bus operations of FCH Haulage, along with some of its bus fleet, were acquired by the London General Omnibus Company in March 1926, being immediately leased to National. The former FCH services became National 52A (Luton-Breachwood Green-Hitchin), 64 (Luton-Cockernhoe-Tea Green) and 65

(Luton-Stopsley-Ramridge End-Tea Green). The alteration of the boundary for National operating 'on behalf of London General' formally took effect from 1 January 1927, when National's services 16B, 51, 52A, 55, 60, 64 and 66 all received 'N' prefixes, whilst new ADC Reliance single-deck buses, provided by London General but carrying National fleet names, began to appear in Langley Street Depot at Luton to work these services. The former National service 65 was withdrawn as it partly operated outside the agreed boundary, whilst former service 61 (Luton-Wheathampstead) became part of a revised (Saturday only) service N8B (St Albans-Wheathampstead - Luton) around this time.

The accommodation at the former Road Motors' garage at Langley Street, Luton had become a major issue, with vehicles having to be parked overnight on adjacent side roads. A large, new bus garage was proposed to occupy a substantial plot of land between Castle Street and Chapel Street in the centre of Luton. The main garage was extended undercover fully between the two parallel streets, with a partially glazed, ridged roof not requiring any intermediate supports. This could accommodate in excess of 100 vehicles, meeting the combined requirements of National's own vehicles for the Luton area and those leased from London General for services south of the town, for which London General allotted the garage code LU. The acquired land included a large open site immediately north of the new garage which had once been the site of a Norman castle, providing for future expansion, with an empty large house, once the home of Luton brewery magnate J.W. Green, occupying a site beyond on top of a raised mound. The latter site was soon acquired by the National Company's staff social club for the building of a canteen and staff welfare area. In view of National's reluctance to invest in garage properties, it is believed that much of the cost for the development came from London General funds. Langley Street garage was retained for storage of withdrawn vehicles until sold to Dunham & Haines Ltd. as a motor vehicle garage during the 1930s.

The acquisition of Road Motors' operations by National had a condition attached that no existing staff would be made redundant, but that was, apparently, ignored by the new owners. The Lamb Brothers, Sidney W. & H.G., were driver and conductor for Road Motors, regularly working the Luton-Markyate service, and resident in Langley Road (now Latimer Road) almost adjacent to the Road Motors' garage in Luton. Only one brother was offered continuing employment by National (it is not recorded which), and both left National to set up their own rival bus business. Two small capacity buses were acquired, although no details have survived, kept in Frank Williams' Excelsior Garage in Albert Road, Luton. They commenced a service in July 1927 in competition with National's service N55 (Luton-Markyate). Lamb Bros.' new service operated between Luton and Slip End, Markyate and Flamstead, although permission to ply for hire was not granted within the Borough of Luton until September. By omitting Woodside, a basic hourly service could be operated by one bus although minimal layovers were scheduled. At peak times, two buses operated alternately over the full route and only as far as Markyate, but without any layover, to provide double the frequency. Unlike National, Lamb Bros. offered cheap return tickets, and cheaper workman's returns for the morning peak trade. Attempts to expand the fleet and operate other services were met with refusals from the Luton Borough Watch Committee, possibly unsure that the Excelsior Garage could accommodate more vehicles. Despite this, the Luton-Flamstead service continued successfully, using the fleet name 'Renown Motor Services'. At some stage, probably to compete more effectively with Renown, National's N55 was diverted to operate directly from Luton to Slip End, via Woodside to Markyate.

The closing months of 1927 brought another major development affecting the area covered in this section. The appearance of modern, pneumatic-tyred, low suspension buses and coaches had resulted in new long-distance coach services, including some regular commuter style services around larger towns and cities, but interestingly not around London. The Public Carriage Office of the Metropolitan Police had laid down strict regulations of the types of vehicle which could ply for hire within their area, which largely precluded the use of coaches on anything other than pre-booked block bookings to and from London. In November 1927, Ralph Priest's 'Imperial Pullman Coaches' of Tottenham cautiously started a 3-times daily (once only on Sunday) coach service between King's Cross (York Road, now York Way) and Luton, Manchester Square, the site of the Galaxy Centre today. Tickets had to be pre-booked at booking agents, which were usually located adjacent to stopping places and the only stopping points within the Metropolitan Police area (as far north as the Colne River in London Colney) were at King's Cross and North Finchley. The vehicles used were Guy coaches described as 'the most luxurious in the country' with individual tables and reading lamps serving each seat. The Metropolitan Police found no reason to object, and the service was considerably increased the following month, then extended to Bedford in February 1928. In December 1927, competition briefly appeared with the introduction of a London coach service from Dunstable Road, Luton, the garage premises of W.T. Parrott & Co. at the top of Beech Hill, into King's Cross, under the title of 'The Beech Hill Safety Coach'. The service survived for just four weeks. Parrott's returned to garage ownership, and later became more successful road hauliers. Elsewhere around the Home Counties, other coach operators quickly followed suit on routes linking the Home Counties with Central London, becoming less cautious about possible police intervention by offering on-vehicle fare collection, more frequent picking up points and more localised fares. Imperial first experienced competition between Bedford and London in June 1928, but their big test for the Luton/Harpenden/St Albans area came in October 1928.

Luton entrepreneur Harry Hill owned a small haulage business and two coaches in cramped premises in Windsor Walk, Luton. He was offered the chance to acquire a large area of land behind premises in the Town Centre off Park Street and Park Street West, opposite J.W. Green's brewery. He built a coach station and a garage large enough for about 30 coaches, with a forecourt opening on to Park Street near Park Square. Trading as Strawhatter Motor Coaches, he commenced a regular daily coach service linking his Coach Station, Harpenden and St Albans with Barnet, North Finchley, Holloway and King's Cross, offering cheap day return tickets between Luton and London at 2/6d, with Imperial charging 3/6d for their day return ticket. Over time, Strawhatter built up a fleet of new Gilford coaches, which eventually numbered almost thirty. During the summer of 1929, Strawhatter added coastal excursions to their offerings, but their London services remained their main focus. The competition forced Imperial into splitting their London service into two in November 1928, Bedford-London via Hitchin and Luton-London via St Albans; competition on both services was intense, and Ralph Priest sold Imperial to Allan Smith, of Holloway, North London in June 1929. Three months later, Birch Bros. Ltd., of Kentish Town, who had been operating regularly between Bedford and London via Hitchin since November 1928, introduced a Kettering to London daily service which stopped intermediately at Wellingborough, Rushden, Bedford, Luton and St Albans, with the London terminus at Oxford Circus. The service was restricted to one journey a day and failed to gain agents to handle the bookings. It was subsequently diverted away from the Luton and St Albans areas, following Birch's more frequent service via Hitchin from December 1929.

Meanwhile, the Official Receiver had seized control of Imperial; Allan Smith, its new owner, was an undischarged bankrupt and should never have been allowed to bid for the company. The London-Luton operations of Imperial passed to Venture Transport (Hendon) Ltd. in December 1929, despite misgivings by that Company's shareholders in the immediate wake of the Wall Street Crash.

At this time, developments also took place on the Dunstable-St Albans-London route. National's local bus service N4 between Dunstable and St Albans, operated from Hatfield Garage, had not proven particularly remunerative, especially to and from Dunstable, and had been reduced to operation only on Wednesday (Dunstable market day), Saturday and Sunday. Dunstable, located on Watling Street, had previously seen many longer-distance charabanc services pick up passengers in the town, these usually being pre-booked passengers travelling to London. However, little is known about these operations and since they were very infrequent, we will not review them here.

The operations of Arthur Blowers' 'Express' have already been referred to in this section. The company operated between St Albans and Dunstable from September 1927, experiencing maintenance issues resulting in the need to hire vehicles, these being sourced from Frank Cobb's 'Albanian' fleet to maintain the service commitments by 1931. In March 1931, Blowers gave up the Dunstable service in favour of Frank Cobb's Albanian, which commenced a regular daily service between St Albans and Dunstable, extended from St Albans to Redbourn. Another of the many St Albans area local bus operators who ventured on to the Dunstable route was garage proprietor Horace Swatman, of the Clock Tower Garage, Verulam Road, St Albans. Trading as 'Renown', he had been attempting to introduce several local bus services in St Albans during early 1929, but eventually gained the necessary permissions to operate between Dunstable and St Albans, doing so from July 1929. This was quickly followed by an extension via Radlett to the Central London Coach Station at Cartwright Gardens, Islington. This service operated four times daily, with a fifth in the late evening on Thursdays. Unfortunately, Swatman also experienced both maintenance and financial problems, and his ambitious coach service became increasingly unreliable during 1930, ceasing soon after. Charles and Arthur Russett (father and son) set up St Albans & District Motor Services in December 1930, to acquire interests in several local bus businesses which had hit financial problems. The Russetts were part of a Bristol family who were prominent in road haulage in Bristol and had briefly run Poole & District Motor Services until its sale to Hants & Dorset Motor Services in September 1930. As part of their St Albans venture, they reintroduced a St Albans-Dunstable bus service in 1931, only to have their licence application subsequently refused by the newly-established Eastern Traffic Commissioners. Their operations elsewhere within the St Albans area usually proved rather more successful.

An 'out of area' operator to feature briefly during 1929 was Bulwark Transports. The Company was based in Archway Road, Highgate, North London, as the Bulwark Manufacturing Co. They had been manufacturing aircraft components since the First World War and diversified into haulage and motor charabanc hire in the early 1920s. Having obtained a new Gilford coach, they introduced a twice-daily motor coach service between Dunstable Square and the Embankment (Charing Cross Underground Station) from Easter 1929, but the entire Bulwark business was a victim of the international financial crisis of October 1929, being put into liquidation on 4 November 1929.

A few months previously, in June, Arthur Priest had commenced a Dunstable-King's Cross coach service under the 'Safeway Coaches' name. Arthur Priest was the elder brother of Ralph Priest, and the two brothers had built up 'Imperial' at Tottenham as a haulage, charabanc hire and London independent bus operator between 1920 and 1927; their partnership was dissolved in summer 1927, after which younger brother Ralph introduced Imperial's pioneer Luton-King's Cross coach service in November 1927. In the meantime, Arthur had attempted, in vain, to establish an operating base in several towns for a business of coach services between the Home Counties and London, using the Safeway Coaches title. In June 1929, he arrived in Dunstable, with limited capital and just one coach. His new service relied heavily on vehicles hired from other operators, especially believed to be Fred England's XL Service, and this became more so subsequently when he obtained permission, with many strings attached, for a King's Cross-Hertford service which required a further coach he simply did not have. His dilemma came to the notice of William Beaumont, a garage proprietor and coach operator, in Enfield, who agreed to provide financial backing and two coaches for Priest's London-Dunstable operations provided he gave up any attempt to operate the London-Hertford service. Under the new title 'Beaumont-Safeway', Arthur Priest set up home in Leighton Buzzard with a small coach garage next to his bungalow and extended the King's Cross to Dunstable service to Leighton Buzzard on certain journeys. For the time being, the business thrived.

Against this increasingly chaotic background, there were moves to enforce regulation on the industry by parliamentary action. Three key Bills affected the industry between 1928 and 1933, especially the area of our study in this section, not helped by frequent changes of government during the same era. The Railways (Road Transport) Act of 1928 legalised something that had been already happening in places for many years. It provided for the four main line railway companies to invest in road haulage or bus operators regardless of whether the road service was provided in connection with railway services. Under the previous legislation, for example, the Great Western Railway had introduced many rural bus services in the South West and in South Wales under the pretext they were in connection with the Company's railway services, yet most of the passengers used them as purely local bus services. Now, a financial link between the main line railway companies and territorial bus companies, or the larger road haulage companies, was seen as a useful way of replacing some unremunerative branch railway lines, or conversely channelling railway companies' large financial reserves into cash-starved bus companies. The National Omnibus & Transport Company clearly saw themselves in the latter category in 1928 and opened an immediate dialogue with each of the big four main line railway companies.

The second Bill to affect the bus industry was the 1930 Road Traffic Act, which, amongst very many other things, transferred regulatory powers from local authorities, where there were major anomalies between adjacent authorities in the way business was handled, to newly-appointed Traffic Commissioners through newly-established Traffic Courts. Bus operators throughout the country had to apply for permission to continue running services many had run for years; those who could afford legal representation sometimes distorted evidence to gain a result in their favour as there was no oath taken nor jury to convince in these Traffic Courts. The third Bill which was particularly relevant to the area southwards from Luton was the London Passenger Transport Act 1933, which established a new state-owned authority to provide all public transport facilities (bus, tram and rail) within an area approximately 25 miles from Charing Cross, with a right to operate such services up to approximately 30 miles from Charing Cross. The Underground Group had been keenly involved in this particular piece of legislation for several years, as they were intent that their Board of Directors should become the Directors of the new London Passenger Transport Board when it was eventually formed. In particular, they were extremely wary of representatives of the big four main line railway companies becoming too involved in this new authority.

As previously mentioned, the arrangements for providing bus services in the Northern Home Counties, made between National and the Underground Group, closely resembled arrangements made between the East Surrey Traction Company and the Underground Group in the Southern Home Counties. When the Railways (Road Transport) Act was passed in 1928, the Southern Railway Company immediately made overtures to East Surrey about a possible acquisition, the Railway Company even registering the Southern General Omnibus Company title as a possible name for the former East Surrey operations. At the time, the Underground Group already held a significant minority shareholding in East Surrey; they acted quickly to secure the support of the Company's long serving Managing Director, Arthur Hawkins, and buy sufficient of his shareholding to give the Underground Group control of East Surrey by 1929. To the North-West of London, financial control of Amersham & District had already passed to the Underground Group by 1930. It was the position of the National Omnibus & Transport Company Ltd., operating services in the Home Counties to the North, North East and East of London, that gave cause for concern, as National were known to be deeply involved in discussion with all four main line railway companies, having registered the names Eastern National, Midland National, Northern National, Southern National and Western National as potential bus company names.

The Underground Group's solution was to wind up the East Surrey Traction Company Ltd., and re-float it as London General Country Services Ltd., acquiring additional services from Woking & District in the process, but with the intention of terminating National's lease of London General's buses and property in the Northern Home Counties, which took effect at the end of January 1932, with the East Surrey Traction Company owning the buses and property to the north of London during the month of February 1932. Staff, leased vehicles and property were eventually transferred to the ownership of London General Country Services Ltd., now a wholly-owned subsidiary of the Underground Group on 1 March 1932, at which time the implementation of the new London Passenger Transport Board (LPTB) was only 16 months distant; it was an interim measure to prevent National's involvement with the main line railway companies, preventing them from gaining influence within the new LPTB. Southern National and Western National took over bus services in the West Country, Devon and Cornwall that lay within areas served by the Southern and Great Western Railways, respectively with significant shareholding in each bus company held by the relevant railway company during 1929 which did not prove an easy task where one bus service passed railway lines of both companies. In the Bedfordshire, Hertfordshire and Essex areas there were railway services provided by both LMS and LNER. To prevent any further messy segregation, all provincial bus services in these areas were transferred during 1930 to the Eastern National Omnibus Company Ltd., in which shareholdings were held by both railway companies, the new bus company having its registered office and main garage at Chelmsford. The exception was the Grays area of Essex, where interworking of National's services made it difficult to segregate operations between those provided directly by National and those on behalf of London General. Here, the status quo was allowed to remain until the London

Passenger Transport Board was established from 1 July 1933. As far as the area south of Luton was concerned, vehicles began appearing with General fleet names, usually on a white background emblem, replacing the National fleet names, but this was only an interim arrangement. At the same time, the use of the 'N' prefixes to the route numbers ended. These had indicated services run on behalf of London General, although older vehicles with service number stencils often continued to display the 'N' for some time. In Hitchin, this created an anomaly as Eastern National had a regular service 52B from Luton to Hitchin, Letchworth and Norton, whilst London General Country Services also operated journeys between Hitchin and Luton, via Breachwood Green, as their service 52B.

Prior to the transfer of bus services to London General Country Services Ltd., National had introduced a new Sunday operation in 1930 by extending the very rural Hitchin-Breachwood Green-Luton service N52A a substantial distance to Dunstable, Well Head, Dagnall, Ashridge and Berkhamsted. The journeys on this service which served the hamlet of Ley Green instead of Whitehall Farm were renumbered N52B about the same time. Following the introduction of the Sunday service, demand for a regular weekday service grew, but only between Dunstable and Berkhamsted, as a new service N52C.

The N55A was another new service introduced, which was the diversion of part of the Luton-Markyate service N55 at the northern end of Markyate High Street, to operate to Kensworth instead of continuing through Markyate. During 1930, competition appeared on National's Saturday only service N16B between Luton, Dunstable, Dunstable Downs and Studham, from a new operator entitled the Union Jack (Luton) Omnibus Company Ltd. Its background was complex and involved many other operations to the north and west of the Luton/Dunstable area.

The operations of Alfred Frederic England have already been touched upon in the National to United Counties section, with further reference being made in the following section, Luton Corporation. It is at this point we should review his operations within the area of study of this section. Alfred 'Fred' purchased a Ford T van which he used to deliver goods in 1922. At the same time, he would use this vehicle to carry fourteen passengers using removeable seats, the vehicle being kept in the Lovers' Walk/Britain Street area of Dunstable. Several small capacity coaches soon replaced the original vehicle. It was in the spring of 1927 that England entered into bus operation when he started the XL Services operation using several French-built Laffley single-deck buses. He commenced operation of a service from Dunstable High Street South/Great Northern Road to Luton Library via Houghton Regis. England gained a reputation for having access to finance which he was willing to invest in other people's bus projects, provided they repaid the loan. Amongst other ventures, he seems to have given financial backing to the Union Jack (Luton) Omnibus Co. Ltd. about 1929-1930. In 1928, there were lucrative openings for unskilled labourers at the Vauxhall Motors plant in Luton, which had recently been acquired by the American General Motors group, provided applicants could travel daily to and from the plant, at the shift working hours stipulated. For many living in the villages of South Bedfordshire, these factors were a major problem, as National's bus service times were unsuitable and their fares prohibitively high for regular daily travel. In 1928, Herbert Witherington, who lodged in the Griffin' Toddington, bought two small single-deck buses to provide a contract-style service between Toddington, nearby villages and the Vauxhall Works in Luton, with fares payable in advance off the vehicle, probably on a weekly basis. At lunchtimes, it is believed he provided much shorter journeys between Vauxhall Works and the nearby Newtown area of Luton, to enable other workers, living nearby, to go home for lunch during their hour's meal break, as the works then had no canteen facilities. By not collecting individual fares, he did not contravene Luton Borough's Watch Committee Regulations for 'plying for hire', but he had formally applied for permission to do so. Unfortunately, after only a brief period of operation, he was observed collecting individual fares from passengers boarding one of his buses in Toddington Road, Leagrave. Witherington was probably unaware that Leagrave was now part of the Borough of Luton, having been incorporated only about a year previously, but was successfully prosecuted for illegally plying for hire within the Borough of Luton, and obliged to withdraw his formal application to do so legally. It is not known whether Witherington's venture had received financial backing from Fred England.

The Union Jack (Luton) Omnibus Company Ltd., registered in October 1928, purchased Witherington's vehicles and, apparently, continued and expanded his bus operations. Its directors were: Frank Williams, proprietor of the Excelsior Garage in Albert Road, Luton, where the new company had their registered office and proposed to keep some of their vehicles; Amos Barber, landlord of the Robin Hood pub in Newtown Street; and Charlie Strapps, landlord of the Rabbit in Old Bedford Road, Luton. It is almost certain that Fred England was involved financially in the new business. It is known that other buses were bought, often being kept overnight in village pub yards, and used for 'contract style' runs to and from Luton Vauxhall. As Vauxhall Works then closed at lunchtime on Saturday, several of the Union Jack vehicles were available for bus work elsewhere on Saturday afternoons, hence the introduction of the Luton-Dunstable-Studham service. The implementation of the 1930 Road Traffic Act required Union Jack to deposit licence applications for proposed bus services, and it is recorded that about sixteen applications were made, usually for services to and from Vauxhall Works which they had been operating on a contract basis, or sometimes they had merely thought of operating. Frank Williams had resigned as a director, and the business's registered office moved from the Excelsior Garage to a solicitor's office in Luton. Suddenly, in March 1931, Fred England announced he was now the owner of the Union Jack (Luton) Omnibus Company Ltd. He failed to locate the business's assets, identifying one bus only, which was parked inside the Excelsior Garage, with two employees, a driver and conductor. He was convinced there were many others in pub yards or farm outbuildings around South Bedfordshire, but they were, apparently, nowhere to be found. He agreed with the East Midland Traffic Commissioners, who were then responsible for the Luton and Dunstable areas, to withdraw all Union Jack's licence applications apart from one for a service between Leighton Buzzard-Luton, Vauxhall and the Saturday afternoon Studham service. Anxious to ease a massive backlog of licence applications, the Commissioners readily agreed, and Fred England then sought to amend the Luton-Studham Saturday service, diverting it to serve Whipsnade Zoo from its opening in May 1931, which the Commissioners also viewed sympathetically. Fred England continued to be involved with XL in Luton, Houghton Regis, Dunstable and parts of the Bedfordshire/Buckinghamshire borders, but also with Herbert Hinds' Blue Bird bus operations in Luton during 1932. He used the Union Jack (Luton) Omnibus Co. Ltd. not only to continue to provide a Saturday afternoon service between Luton, Dunstable and Whipsnade Zoo, but also to purchase vehicles for the cash-starved Blue Bird fleet, to buy out several operators in Bedford, and finally to acquire and expand the Renown business of the Lamb Bros.

There were other significant developments during 1930 which would affect the area south of Luton and Dunstable. To combat the tremendous growth of coach services linking the Home Counties with Central London during 1929, many of which were probably destined to be refused licences by the newly-appointed Traffic Commissioners as unnecessary new services, the Underground Group proposed their own network of limited stop coach services extending up to 30 miles from Central London, and often linked across London to reduce parking problems for coaches during layovers there. It was stressed that these services would operate on a regular frequency throughout the day, not just at peak times as many of the rival commuter services operated. At a management presentation in early 1930, the proposed services were shown in green on an enlarged map of the Home Counties area and were referred to as 'these Green Lines', giving birth to the fleet name. The coaches to work these services would be based at garages under National or East Surrey control where appropriate, but sometimes it was necessary to use a third party's premises, or even provide a new garage, under the auspices of a new Underground Group Company, Green Line Coaches Ltd.

The Green Line network began to appear during 1930, although several existing coach services linking Watford with Golders Green and Central London, which had been introduced by London General during 1929, were incorporated into the Green Line network the following year. The first appearance of a Green Line coach service in the Luton and Dunstable area took place on 20 September 1930, when a new daily service commenced between Harpenden and Embankment (Charing Cross Underground Station), via St Albans, Radlett, Watford Way, Mill Hill and Golders Green. Operated by Green Line Coaches Ltd., the new 27-seat AEC Regal coaches were garaged at 'Comfy Car's' new garage on the corner of Harpenden High Street and Townsend Lane, where the premises were far larger than required for the four Comfy Car coaches. Due to the popularity of the existing Strawhatter and Venture coach services which already linked Luton with London, and picked up in Harpenden and St Albans, the decision was taken to curtail the Green Line service at Harpenden at this stage. It was also decided that no Green Line service to Redbourn, Markyate or Dunstable could be justified at this time. The policy to link Green Line services across Central London was then enacted, and the Harpenden service was extended from Embankment to Great Bookham, via Epsom and Leatherhead from 10 December 1930, replacing a Great Bookham-Oxford Circus service which had commenced on 1 October 1930. The Green Line services were identified by service letters from late February 1931, with the Harpenden-Great Bookham service becoming service H.

The applications for Road Service Licences from the newly initiated Traffic Courts commenced their hearings in Spring 1931, destined to continue for several years simply to establish the status quo. There were no controversial decisions affecting the services within the area under study, once Fred England had struck his deal with the Commissioners over Union Jack's applications, unlike many of the surrounding areas. As these got under way, the opening of Whipsnade Zoo took place on Whitsun weekend in May 1931, with road access to the area severely hampered by delayed completion of road widening and construction work on new roads within the main access areas. In particular, delays in completion of the road linking Kensworth Common Road with Whipsnade Common meant that road traffic inward from Watling Street and the south was diverted at Markyate along the narrow lane directly to Whipsnade Common, whilst return traffic was diverted via the southern end of Dunstable Downs and the single-track Isle of Wight Lane. On the opening day, Whit

Saturday, bad weather kept the crowds away, but the following two days, Whit Sunday and Bank Holiday Monday, brought fine weather, unexpectedly large crowds, and traffic jams on a scale previously unseen in the area. Eastern National bore the brunt of the visitors' traffic, with their new service 53B from Station Road, Luton via Dunstable and Dunstable Downs having to be much augmented to cope with the crowds and delays due to the severe traffic jams. Eastern National had also implemented country services from Bedford and Leighton Buzzard direct to Whipsnade Zoo, but these tended to be under-utilised with visitors preferring to travel via Luton or Dunstable. The service from Leighton Buzzard was eventually a wartime cut which never returned.

National's initial operations to Whipsnade Zoo were more affected by the failure to complete road construction work. Most journeys on service N55A (Luton-Kensworth) were 'extended' daily from Kensworth to Whipsnade Zoo, but the outward journeys to the Zoo could not serve Kensworth until the new road between Kensworth and Whipsnade Cross Roads had been constructed. The extension to Whipsnade Zoo, which did not apply to all journeys, operated daily during the summer timetable, but was restricted to weekends and holidays only during the winter timetable. National also served Whipsnade Zoo by a new limited stop coach service from Rickmansworth, Watford and Hemel Hempstead, which appears to have been allocated service letter 'Z' in the Green Line series, although there is no evidence it was ever operated under the Green Line name. At the end of the 1931 summer season, service Z was withdrawn to be partially replaced by journeys on the Watford-Bovingdon-Hemel Hempstead service N17, which was extended from Hemel Hempstead to Whipsnade Zoo, these journeys later being renumbered as service N16. No service appears to have been offered initially linking Whipsnade Zoo with the Redbourn and St Albans area, nor with Central London.

A 'true' Green Line service to Whipsnade Zoo was eventually introduced in late March 1932 as new service BH operating between Baker Street Station and Whipsnade Zoo via St Albans and Redbourn, although the London terminus quickly moved to Marylebone Station forecourt, to accommodate the excessive queues waiting at Bank Holiday times. A fleet of new AEC Regal T type coaches was moved into the empty London General garage in Leavesden Road, Watford to provide this service.

Green Line's other operation in the area, service H between Harpenden and Great Bookham, remained with Harpenden as its northern terminus because of the competition from the Strawhatter and Venture coach services between Luton and King's Cross. Of these two, Strawhatter had the upper hand, but a co-ordinated timetable and fare-table had been agreed from March 1932, although Venture, with fewer journeys, still ran from Manchester Square in Luton whilst Strawhatter ran from their Coach Station off Park Square. In August 1932, the Underground Group, through Green Line Coaches Ltd., made a bid of £30,000 for the Strawhatter business, which Harry Hill regarded as insulting and chose to ignore. With the London Passenger Transport Act taking effect from mid-1933, Venture were increasingly uneasy about the future of the Luton-London coach service, although their journeys were technically 'safe' as the Manchester Square terminus was just outside the proposed London Transport operating area, and therefore were not liable for compulsory purchase. Nevertheless, Harry Hill agreed to purchase the Venture operations on the Luton to London service, Strawhatter becoming the sole operator from 1 January 1933. No vehicles were acquired, Strawhatter buying more new Gilford coaches to work the former Venture journeys. Venture continued their other coach operations in the

Hendon area. The former Venture journeys still continued to use Manchester Square as the Luton terminus.

Strawhatter's London service continued to show a significant profit, and Harry Hill actually hoped that the new London Transport would attempt to make a compulsory purchase order for Strawhatter, since the arbitration procedures included in the Act should have given a very substantial price for the business. With a registered office and operating base outside the 'Special Area' and part of his operations, the former Venture journeys and the summer coastal work, partly outside the London Transport operating area, compulsory acquisition terms should not have applied to the Strawhatter business. Nevertheless, the Board did invoke compulsory purchase terms to acquire the Strawhatter business, including its coastal express, excursions, garage and coach station, and small road haulage business from 1 February 1934, with a proposed financial settlement of £57,000, which was rejected out of hand.

Eight of the twenty-four Gilford coaches were immediately handed over to the Eastern National Omnibus Company Ltd., together with the licences to operate the summer coastal express services to Great Yarmouth, Margate, Portsmouth & Southsea and Bournemouth, and a number of excursion & tours destinations. The cash settlement for this transfer, details of which remained commercially confidential, was not agreed until May 1934. The road haulage operations, involving three lorries, continued to be operated by London Transport until sold to Pickfords Ltd. on 21 June 1934 for £662. The Luton terminus for the former Venture journeys to London was immediately moved to the Park Street coach station, and the Luton to King's Cross coach service became Green Line service BH. The cheap day return fares to and from King's Cross remained in force for many years afterwards, the fares being much cheaper than equivalent distance fares elsewhere on Green Line. Frank Pick was only too well aware of a potential scandal should the new Board immediately enforce a fare increase.

Space was made at the former Strawhatter coach station, with the undercover area becoming the main London Transport garage for Luton. The London General Country Service vehicles that had previously been housed at Castle Street, Luton (LU), were transferred to the former Strawhatter premises which gained code LS (Luton, Strawhatter). Over the coming years, the garage was gradually rebuilt. The majority of the open forecourt facing Park Street, latterly used as the coach station, was sold for redevelopment of new retail outlets. The Green Line stands were eventually moved on to Park Street itself, where the country bus services already terminated, whilst the former garage entrance was reduced to just a fire exit. A new main entrance was provided from Park Street West, facing J.W. Green's brewery, by cutting an archway into the 3-storey building terrace, and acquiring adjoining 3-storey terraced houses for conversion into enquiry office, staff canteen and administrative offices. After rejection of the £57,000 offer, a 'final offer' of £65,000 was made, and also immediately rejected, as was a further 'final offer' of £80,000. At this point, during summer 1935, the results of arbitration awards for other acquired businesses became known, and most had not gone in the Board's favour. Harry Hill now indicated he was seeking arbitration, panicking the Board into offering £97,500 which was accepted by Hill in August 1935.

Returning to the Luton-Flamstead operation of the Luton-based Lamb Bros. who were trading as Renown, we encounter Fred England once again in early 1933. As mentioned previously, the Lamb Bros. had been frustrated in their attempts to expand their operations by Luton Borough's refusal to licence more than two vehicles to ply for hire, in particular to operate duplicate vehicles at peak times. Fred England's empire had grown to include XL Service and Blue Bird, both outside the area under review in this section, as well as the Luton-Whipsnade Zoo Saturday service operated by one vehicle under the Union Jack banner. He was probably surprised that Eastern National showed no interest in acquiring his business and offered the three businesses instead to Luton Corporation Transport. Although agreement on the sale was quickly reached in October 1932, it took until March 1933 before the details were legally finalised and most of England's Luton area operations and most of his fleet of buses passed to Luton Corporation Transport on 23 March 1933. As far as the south Luton area was concerned, the former Union Jack Luton-Dunstable-Whipsnade service was curtailed to run between Luton-Dunstable only under the control of Luton Corporation Transport, leaving Eastern National's 53B as the sole service over the busy link from Luton via Dunstable.

Whilst awaiting the conclusion of the sale, Fred England had used the anticipated finances to buy part of the Carding family's bus business in Kempston, Bedford, and then, on 27 March 1933, to buy Lamb Bros.' Renown business based in Luton, with its vehicle-starved Luton-Flamstead bus service. Both acquisitions had been carried out by the Union Jack (Luton) Omnibus Co. Ltd., now based in the former stable yard behind his father's bakery off High Street South in Dunstable, but with an outstation leased at Bedford in the yard of the Simplex works on Elstow Road. No vehicles were acquired from Renown, with Union Jack now purchasing several Dennis 30-seat single-deck buses through a London dealer, originally used by Birch Bros. Ltd., on some of their London suburban bus services, but considered surplus to requirements by the LPTB. The scheduled service on Luton-Flamstead remained unchanged from that advertised by Lamb Bros., but it's clear the level of duplication at peak times increased dramatically under Union Jack operation. In 1936, Eastern National purchased the operations of Lamb Bros. from A.F. England.

The London Passenger Transport Board (LPTB) commenced operation on 1 July 1933, with the acquisition of the major London bus and tram operators, together with almost all the underground railway network. The effect it had on the focus area of this section was the services operated by London General Country Services Ltd. (LGCS) generally passed to LPTB on the due date, with some minor changes taking place. The new Board continued to acquire other bus operators within their area during the ensuing 18 months. Pressure from Luton Corporation had resulted in a clause inserted in the London Passenger Transport Act forbidding the new Board from carriage of local passengers within the Borough of Luton. This was carried forward into the London Transport Executive in 1948 and was not revoked until about 1964. Fourteen services operating in the area concerned passed to London Transport. These were LGCS 4 (Dunstable-St Albans), 8B (Luton–Wheathampstead-St Albans), 16 (Watford-Hemel Hempstead-Whipsnade Zoo), 16B (Dunstable-Studham), 51 (Luton–Harpenden-St Albans), 52A/B (Luton-Breachwood Green-Hitchin via Whitehall or Ley Green), 52C (Dunstable–Dagnall-Berkhamsted), 55 (Luton-Markyate), 55A (Luton-Kensworth or Whipsnade Zoo), 60 (Luton-Caddington), 64 (Luton-Tea Green), Green Line H (Harpenden-Great Bookham), and Green Line BH (Whipsnade Zoo-Marylebone). The Luton-Dunstable section of service 16B and the Sunday operation on services 52A/B were immediately withdrawn as outside the LPTB's Operating Area. Service 52C gained a Sunday service between Dunstable and Berkhamsted as a result. The ban on local carriage within the Borough of Luton most affected the Farley Hill section of services 55/A and 60, and the Crawley Green Road section of service 64; in both cases, new housing development had forced Luton Corporation Transport to provide new bus services from autumn 1932 to cover the eventual loss of the LGCS services.

In October 1933, whilst Strawhatter Coaches remained independent, London Transport reorganised all Green Line coach services, to provide a greater degree of cross-London links and more economical operation of existing services. Service H from Harpenden was relinked across London to operate to East Grinstead instead of Great Bookham, whilst the Whipsnade Zoo-Marylebone service, formerly BH, now became service U. At the same time, a new Green Line service AH was introduced between Dunstable and East Grinstead, which was combined with the existing service H to provide a double frequency between St Albans and East Grinstead. This did not bode well for the final remaining express coach between London and Dunstable, the King's Cross-Dunstable-Leighton Buzzard service of Beaumont-Safeway. Having been a relative newcomer to the London-Dunstable route in late 1929, their application to the Metropolitan Traffic Commissioner for an express carriage licence had not been well received, and the licence granted already virtually prohibited carriage of most intermediate passengers south of Dunstable. The new Green Line service threatened their London to Dunstable trade as well. Although the financial partnership between William Beaumont and Arthur Priest was dissolved, Arthur Priest continued to act as Beaumont's manager at Leighton Buzzard, whilst Beaumont sought to sell the business to London Transport. With the Leighton Buzzard operating base some eight miles outside London Transport's operating area, London Transport showed little interest, but eventually agreed to buy the business for a meagre offer, which had to be accepted by Beaumont towards the end of April 1934. The Beaumont journey times were abandoned, the new Green Line AH covering as far as Dunstable, whilst the Leighton Buzzard journeys were abandoned without replacement.

The independent operators based in St Albans, Boxmoor and Berkhamsted but running into the area of study were largely absorbed into the new Board's operations during 1933/4. S.H. Viles' Pioneer Bus Service of Berkhamsted, operating to Dunstable via Hemel Hempstead on Wednesdays, Saturdays and Sundays, was acquired by London Transport during 1934, its service becoming London Transport route 319; by this time, the eventual renumbering of London Transport's Country Bus Services in the northern area into the 300 series had been decided, although not actioned. Acquired unnumbered services were immediately allocated vacant numbers in the 300 series. Similarly, West Herts Motor Services, of Boxmoor, was acquired in 1934 and its service from Boxmoor Station to Hemel Hempstead, which extended at weekends to Gaddesden Row and Dunstable, became route 337. On the Dunstable-St Albans road, the acquisition of Cobbs' Albanian by London Transport on 17 February 1934 included that service between Dunstable and St Albans. For a short time, this service was incorporated into service 4. On the Luton-St Albans road, the Morgan Bros' Comfy Car service was acquired by London Transport in February 1934, to become part of service 51, together with the garage premises in Harpenden High Street. After a number of years of close co-operation between Comfy Car and London Transport, LGCS, National and even Road Motors, the end proved acrimonious. London Transport's compulsory purchase offer of £8,500 for the business was considered derisory. Although the final settlement (£15,500), in 1936, was much in favour of Comfy Car, Philip Morgan had died in the meantime, leaving only brother Alfred to reap the benefit, in retirement in Sussex. The journeys between St Albans (Fleetville) and Luton operated by Blowers' Express passed to London Transport with the Express business on 2 January 1934, also becoming part of service 51.

On 3 October 1934, the bus services within both Central Bus and Country Bus Areas were renumbered to introduce the area scheme, whereby all Country Bus Services would be numbered in the 300 or 400 series according to whether located in the Northern or Southern Areas. The renumbering of services within the area of study involved service 4 (Dunstable-St Albans) which became service 374, service 8B (Luton-Wheathampstead-St Albans) becoming service 365. Service 16 (Watford-Whipsnade Zoo) was renumbered 367, whilst service 51 (Luton-Harpenden-St Albans) became service 321A. Service 52A (Luton-Breachwood Green-St Albans) was numbered 383, whilst service 52C (Dunstable-Dagnall-Berkhamsted) became the 352. Service 55 (Luton-Markyate) became service 356, whilst service 55A (Luton-Kensworth/Whipsnade Zoo) was renumbered 376. Service 60 (Luton-Caddington) became service 360, and service 64 (Luton-Tea Green) gained service number 364. Services 319 and 337 have already been mentioned, although the former service 16B (Dunstable-Studham) was merged into service 337 to provide a more regular through service between Boxmoor and Dunstable. By this date, there were also weekday peak hour journeys between Dunstable and Kensworth, which now operated under service 374, although the diversion to serve Kensworth was off the normal line of route. The former service 52B journeys via Whitehall Farm had now all been diverted to serve Ley Green and were included in service 383.

The rolling stock used at this time on most of the London Transport Country Bus Services in the area under review was predominantly the ADC 416 single-deck, which gained classification code 'R'. However, some of the former Strawhatter Gilfords were also in use, which became known as the 'GF' class, these being mainly used on bus work. Green Line services H, AH and U retained the 'T' class AEC Regals with the former Strawhatter Gilfords being used on service BH.

19 September 1934 saw Green Line route H extended from Harpenden to Luton, Park Square; it continued to be operated from Harpenden Garage, as there was no spare capacity in Luton. Whilst fares on route H had to be in line with those on BH, there is no doubt most passengers travelling from Luton, Harpenden or St Albans towards London at this time still preferred to use route BH. During 1935, the West Hyde-Watford-St Albans route 321 was extended to Harpenden and Luton to replace route 321A. This brought regular double-deck operation back to the St Albans-Luton road, initially in the guise of ST-class vehicles, but these were soon replaced by new forward-entrance STL-class vehicles, based at both Watford High Street (WT) and Luton (LS). At this time, local bus trade had declined between Dunstable and St Albans, resulting in route 374 being cut back from Dunstable to mostly operate between St Albans and Redbourn. Some peak-time journeys were extended to Friars Wash, and a few to Markyate. To compensate for the loss of the Dunstable to St Albans section, Green Line route AH began to serve all bus stops on this section. This is believed to be the first such arrangement made for a Green Line service to act as a 'normal' country bus over a lightly-trafficked section of route. The Kensworth-Dunstable peak hour journeys, previously worked as route 374, were now renumbered 376A. As part of a gradual scheme to amend the Green Line letter identities to alphanumeric, routes H and AH became H1 and H2 from 8 January 1936, but route BH did not become route H3 until 29 July 1936. Early 1936 saw the opening of a new garage at St Albans, which was allocated depot code SA, with many services previously operated from Hatfield (HF) now operating from there, often using double-deck ST and STLs. The older Strawhatter Gilfords used on bus work were sold about this time, replaced at Luton by T-class AEC Regals dating back to 1931, new to Queen

Line, formerly Baldock Motor Transport, with coach bodies built by London Lorries, which did not wear well. These had been acquired by Green Line Coaches Ltd. in April 1933, already in dubious condition, and were rebodied with new Weymann single-deck bus bodies in 1935-6, after which they were allocated to Luton for bus work. The former Strawhatter Gilfords still in use on Green Line coach work were transferred to Romford (RE) in 1936, to join the many former Hillman Coaches' Gilfords already there. Their place at Luton were probably filled by new T-class saloons of the 9T9 model, these later being demoted to bus work.

1936 saw the Luton-Markyate-Flamstead service continue under the operation of Fred England's Union Jack (Luton) Omnibus Company, along with a number of services in the Bedford area. Several years previously, Frank Pick had decided not to pursue Union Jack as an acquisition for London Transport, but now he was under pressure from Eastern National to reconsider as they were anxious to acquire England's Bedford area operations, and he would not sell one part of the business without the other. Eventually, the entire Union Jack business was acquired by Eastern National from 9 December 1936 for a sum of £25,000, the Luton to Flamstead service becoming Eastern National's service 83. By prior agreement, the latter service passed to London Transport, without any vehicles, after three months, taking place in March 1937, in which relative revenue figures were obtained, with the Luton-Flamstead service now becoming London Transport route 356A. London Transport paid £8,000 for their share of the Union Jack business, although Frank Pick had estimated it was worth only £3,000 and he was not amused by Eastern National's handling of the acquisition. Traffic along the Luton-Markyate corridor was growing steadily at this time, and regular double-deck workings were scheduled on route 356, with at least one ST allocated full-time at Luton for this purpose. Around this time a new bus service to Whipsnade Zoo was introduced from St Albans via Redbourn and Markyate, numbered 368.

By 1938, the establishment of the Empire Rubber Company's factory, and an associated housing estate for workers about two miles south of Dunstable Town Centre, well beyond the Great Northern Road terminus of Luton Corporation's service 6, which was the nearest local bus, must have brought substantial local bus traffic to the Dunstable end of Green Line H2, but London Transport's only local bus service along this section of road remained the few peak hour journeys on route 376A. The summer timetable for 1938 brought a substantial change to the service pattern. The Luton-Markyate route 356 was extended as a regular service to Flamstead, Friar's Wash, Redbourn and St Albans, replacing routes 356A and 374. It is believed it was converted to double-deck operation, using STL types allocated to Luton and St Albans. At the same time, the Luton to Caddington route 360 was converted to double-deck operation, but still only operating about five or six times a day. The local service into Dunstable along the A5, however, remained for most of the day in the hands of Green Line H2. It is also believed that the Hemel Hempstead-Dunstable routes 319 and 337 were rationalised as route 337 only which ran between Boxmoor and Dunstable at this time.

Meanwhile, on the eastern side of the area covered in this section, Arthur Hancock's Whitwell Bus Service business was acquired by Birch Bros. Ltd. from 31 March 1938, as part of the latter company's reinvestment of funds derived from the acquisition of their London local bus operations by London Transport in 1934. The Whitwell-Luton service was allocated number 204, and was increased to a daily service, operating between Hitchin, Whitwell and Luton from March 1939. It was destined to be short-lived, as the service was split in two, with the Whitwell-Luton section again reduced to three days a week as a wartime measure from 15 September 1939.

The Second World War took its toll on the London Transport network in the area of study. From 1 September 1939, all Green Line operations ceased to enable the vehicles used to be fitted as emergency ambulances. Amongst the sections of road identified as requiring immediate additional buses was the A5 Watling Street between the Packhorse at Kensworth Turn and Dunstable, especially as the Empire Rubber Company was now considered an essential plant for the war effort. An unnumbered 'Special Service', operated by single-deck from Luton garage, ran between the Packhorse and Dunstable Square for the following few weeks. Two weeks later, the first wartime emergency timetables brought a new daily, double-deck route 369 between St Albans and Dunstable. The Special Service and route 368 were withdrawn, and route 356 was curtailed to operate between Luton, Markyate and Flamstead only, with some journeys reverting to single-deck operation. Routes 360, 364, 365, 376, 376A and 383 continued largely unchanged, although the Whipsnade Zoo journeys on route 376 were substantially reduced in number.

The beginning of November 1939 saw some Green Line services reinstated, albeit on a limited scale. However, it was not until 7 February 1940 that a service was reinstated in the Luton and Dunstable areas, this being the Luton to Victoria section of route H1. The through service to East Grinstead followed five weeks later on 13 March 1940, the service then being re-lettered as route H. The Green Line services to Dunstable and Whipsnade Zoo, which remained open to the public, were not reinstated. From 23 October 1940, route H was split into two parts at Victoria, to reduce effects of delays due to air raid activity and reduce drivers' hours of continuous driving during blackout periods. From 4 December 1940, the Green Line network was further enlarged, with routes now allocated route numbers. The northern end of route H, Victoria-Radlett-Luton, became route 45, and the former H3 route was reinstated and revised as new route 46 between Luton, Barnet and Victoria. The provision of the reinstated Green Line services placed a strain on single-deck vehicle resources at Luton, and a batch of single-deck Tilling-Stevens buses were hired from United Counties for use at Luton during 1941/42. A growing shortage of fuel supplies brought further withdrawal of all Green Line services after 29 September 1942, for the duration of the remaining war years.

There was some respite from wartime travel demands. In spring 1942, Luton Corporation were able to extend some journeys on their service 6 (Luton-Houghton Regis-Dunstable) from Great Northern Road in Dunstable to the Empire Rubber Company, both at works times and a few 'shopping' journeys for residents of the nearby housing estate. As a security measure, the terminus at the Empire Rubber Company was called 'Kensworth Lane' on destination displays, as a single-track lane led to the isolated Kensworth Parish Church on the opposite side of Watling Street to the factory. There was no road called 'Kensworth Lane' but its use on Luton area destination displays continued until the 1970s. The demands on routes 369 and 376A in Dunstable where longer distance travellers could find difficulty in boarding due to very local passengers, now eased as a result. In May 1943, the need to extend the grass runway at Luton Airport to enable larger aircraft to be built at the Percival plant meant the direct road between Vauxhall Works at Luton and Dane Street, through Spittlesea Woods, would be closed permanently from the following month. Bus routes affected were London Transport 383 (Luton-Breachwood Green-Hitchin), Birch route 204 (Luton-Whitwell) and Jones' Enterprise (Luton-Kimpton-Welwyn). The diversions introduced in June 1943 involved London Transport's 383 and Birch's 204 diverting via Eaton Green Road, and Wigmore Bottom to Breachwood Green. Birch's 204 then continued to Bendish and Whitwell, both routes no longer serving Danestreet, whilst

Enterprise diverted via Newmill End and Chiltern Green. However, it was discovered that Birch were undercutting London Transport's fares on the diversion route. At the same time Hertfordshire County Council were critical of the size of buses being used by Birch on the narrow lanes. Therefore, Birch were instructed to divert the 204 via Newmill End and Chiltern Green, continuing to serve Danestreet but not Breachwood Green. This alteration took effect in September 1943, when London Transport also simplified its services in the area. Routes 364 and 383 were merged under the former route number, to operate as one through service from Luton, running via the Vauxhall Works, Eaton Green Road, Wigmore Bottom, Cockernhoe, Tea Green, Breachwood Green, Kings Walden, Ley Green and Preston to Hitchin.

On 15 June 1944, operation of the Luton-Kimpton-Welwyn bus service was transferred from Enterprise to Birch Bros. Ltd., for an agreed sum. Jones had been experiencing difficulties in recruiting drivers to cover both his bus service and a number of school contract commitments and was somewhat forced into the deal by the Regional Transport Commissioner. He retained both the coaches and school contracts. Birch Bros. Ltd. numbered the service 205 and operated it mainly from an outstation in Dickinson & Adams' car park off Bridge Street, Luton. The level of service provided soon increased substantially over that latterly run by Enterprise. July 1944 saw the demand for additional morning works journeys into Dunstable from the Studham, Whipsnade and Kensworth areas, which could not be met by London Transport, who simply did not have spare road staff available for the extra journeys on routes 337 and 376A. Therefore, Luton Corporation Transport agreed to provide the additional bus needed to operate a weekday peak service between Luton and Studham, via Dunstable, Kensworth and Whipsnade Cross Roads. Initially to be numbered as new service 25, it appeared in July 1944 as extra journeys on their Luton-Dunstable direct service 5, operating on a Defence Permit which had to be renewed annually. In the summer of 1945, a twice-weekly visitors' service was required to link Dunstable with Ashridge Memorial Hospital. Luton Corporation Transport again offered to provide the facility, but London Transport considered this was now within their resources, the new service appeared as Wednesday and Sunday route 352A (Dunstable-Dagnall-Ashridge Memorial Hospital).

The restoration of the Green Line network post-war commenced in February 1946, with a few services added to the network each month until it was complete in July. The services were renumbered into the 700 series. The first to affect the study area was new route 727 operating between King's Cross, Barnet and Luton, recommencing on 1 May 1946. The route was operated from Luton using TF-class Leyland Tiger single-decks, an experimental underfloor-engine vehicle which had been introduced to London Transport in 1938/39. They were mostly used on East London Green Line services pre-war. Four weeks later, on 29 May 1946, new Green Line routes 712 (Dorking-Epsom-Victoria-Radlett-Luton), 713 (Dorking-Epsom-Victoria-Radlett-Dunstable) and 726 (Marylebone-Whipsnade Zoo) (summer only) commenced operation. Routes 712 and 713 were worked by T-class AEC Regals from Dorking and St Albans garages, whilst route 726 operated from Watford, Leavesden Road (WT) using similar vehicles. It was proposed that a new Green Line route 719 would be introduced in July or August 1946, at the end of the programme, as a semi-orbital service linking Luton, St Albans, Watford, Uxbridge, Slough and Windsor to augment existing local bus services which were being increasingly used by longer distance passengers. The plans were dropped after it was discovered that both Luton and Windsor garages did not have the staff to operate this service without reducing other local routes, such as the 321 and 457.

During 1946, Birch Bros. Ltd. had intentions to develop services within the Luton/ Hitchin/Welwyn triangle with regular, daily services on route 205 (Luton-Kimpton-Welwyn) and 206 (Luton-Whitwell-Welwyn), both intended for extension to Welwyn Garden City Station, or, at least, Welwyn North Station. Unfortunately, London Transport blocked both proposals, as they had an earlier, less firm proposal to extend route 205 to Hatfield Station, whilst the bad weather during winter 1946-7 killed much of the remaining trade on these very rural services. During 1947, route 206 was reduced to a Saturday & Sunday operation, with three journeys between Luton & Whitwell only on Thursday, whilst the timetable on route 205 was again reduced, but John Birch would persevere with his proposals during the 1950s.

Meanwhile, the post-war London Transport route network now included route 321 operating between Luton and Uxbridge via Harpenden, St Albans, Watford and Rickmansworth, but, in fact, no journeys covered the full route, with most journeys to and from Luton operating only as far as West Hyde, later extended to Maple Cross. The forward-entrance STL vehicles used on the route since the mid-1930s were largely displaced elsewhere during 1946/47 by the delivery of 30 new AEC Regent II double-deck vehicles, allocated fleet numbers at the end of the STL class, with provincial-style Weymann bodies, which had been allocated to London Transport because of continuing delays in the delivery of new RT-class double-deck buses. These post-war STLs were allocated initially to both Luton and Watford. Under the transport proposals of the Labour Government, the London Passenger Transport Board was abolished after 31 December 1947, replaced by a new London Transport Executive, directly responsible to the Ministry of Transport, and with even greater powers.

Whipsnade Zoo had grown in popularity post-war resulting in the reinstatement of the extensions of most daytime journeys on route 376 from Kensworth during the summer months, but only at weekends during the winter. As a summer only operation, the Enfield to St Albans route 313 was extended to Whipsnade Zoo at weekends and on Bank Holidays. No direct service was reinstated from Hemel Hempstead or Watford in post-war days, but Green Line route 726 gained popularity. For the 1948 summer season, it was converted to double-deck operation. The only garage then using double-deck buses in Green Line livery was Romford, with its fleet of double-deck D-class Daimlers delivered in 1946; these worked route 726 from March 1948, running dead between Romford and a relocated London terminus at Baker Street Station. In time, the Daimlers were replaced by new RT vehicles in Green Line livery with high ratio back axles. It was frequently necessary to operate convoys of vehicles on route 726 on peak summer weekends or Bank Holidays.

The peak-time journeys on Luton Corporation's route 5 operating out to Studham ceased after 31 July 1950, when London Transport increased and extended the peak-hour journeys on the 376A to operate between Studham or Whipsnade and Dunstable, via Kensworth and the A5. Its Dunstable terminus was located either at the Waterlow's Works off Ashton Road, or at A.C. Sphinx at the north end of the town. The closure of part of Judd Street Coach Station at King's Cross after 29 September 1951 resulted in the withdrawal of the Luton-King's Cross Green Line route 727, this being replaced by the extension of the Dorking-Kingston-Baker Street route 714 to Barnet, St Albans and Luton. Route 714 was jointly worked by Dorking and Luton. At this time the TF and T-class vehicles employed on Green Line work were displaced by new RF-class AEC Regal IV underfloor-engine vehicles during 1951-52. The displaced vehicles often ending their days on Country Bus work from either Luton or St Albans garages. From Whitsun 1954, some of the Romford garage journeys on route 726 were to be made in service, the route now operating Romford-Baker Street-St Albans-Whipsnade Zoo, still restricted to summer only and passengers to and from Whipsnade Zoo only. During 1954, the post-war STLs at Luton were displaced to Hertford for use on route 327 which encountered a weak bridge, these vehicles being lighter than RTs. They were replaced at Luton by new RT-class double-decks, these also replacing RF-class single-deck buses which had not long entered service on the 356 and 376. By this means, London Transport justified a near 50 per cent reduction in scheduled service on these increasingly busy routes!

In November 1954, John Birch commenced his new attempt to provide a frequent, regular service between Luton and Welwyn Garden City, via either Kimpton (route 205) or Whitwell (route 206). The Metropolitan Traffic Commissioner was unimpressed by the timetable suggested at the first application and rejected the proposal. Behind the scenes, London Transport were involved in a proposal to double the Green Line service to Hitchin, which would contravene a ruling by the Amulree Committee in 1932 restricting the Green Line service to Hitchin to hourly. John Birch agreed not to object to the Hitchin Green Line proposal if London Transport withdrew their objection to Birch Bros. Ltd. entering Welwyn Garden City with a revised, much increased, timetable. On 22 May 1955, Birch 205 and 206 were both extended from Welwyn to Welwyn Garden City Station. Restrictions were placed on the carriage of local passengers at the Garden City end. London Transport did not increase the Green Line service from Hitchin, but eventually introduced an additional route, 716A, from Stevenage. During the rest of 1955, Birch Bros. Ltd. drew up new schedules for routes 205 and 206 increasing the schedules further and further. A new daily route, 215, was also proposed, linking Luton with Stevenage via Kimpton, Codicote, Knebworth and the Broadwater Estate. London Transport and United Counties objected to the latter, and it was only eventually approved as a very cut down service, operating four days per week between Luton and the Broadwater Estate only, commencing in June 1956. By this time, John Birch had realised the anticipated popularity of Welwyn Garden City was not materialising, and schedules for routes 205 and 206 were being steadily reduced. When Birch Bros. Ltd. applied to halve the already limited service on route 215 in October 1956, London Transport demanded it be withdrawn completely. The Suez Crisis intervened, and fuel rationing cuts were demanded nationally. The Birch cuts involved the Luton-Welwyn Garden City operation being restricted to route 205 only, with routes 206 and 215 both suspended. These would take effect from 7 January 1957, to avoid disruption of Christmas shopping and January sales' trade. When fuel rationing ended in April 1957, neither route returned; the suspensions had become permanent.

Further issues were experienced on the Welwyn Garden City routes. From late 1954, one-man-operation on single-decks seating forty-five or less could be introduced on routes 205 and 206. However, Birch had found that their drivers were unwilling to volunteer unless longer running times were introduced. The route followed between Welwyn and Welwyn Garden City by 205, and 206 when it was running, was lengthy, running via Valley Road with a ban on local traffic. There were also peak hour journeys from Hitchin to Welwyn Garden City's industrial estate worked by Birch as part of their route 204, but on which a minimum fare was charged, rather than an outright ban on local passengers. Now, there was a brand-new road, the redeveloped Digswell Lane, which could be used between Welwyn Garden City and Welwyn, cutting nearly 2 miles off the route. This would doubtless persuade the Birch drivers to accept one-man operation, with an appropriate hourly bonus. London Transport would only accept use of this diversion if the peak hour journeys' restriction, on the Hitchin journeys on route 204, was brought in line with the much tighter restrictions on route 205, which John Birch refused to do. When some level of compromise was reached at the end of 1957, a further dispute flared between the Development Corporation, who refused to accept responsibility for maintenance of the new Digswell Lane, and the contractors, who then refused permission for its use for a regular bus service. Although a new alternative route was identified, John Birch had had enough. He announced the complete withdrawal of route 205 between Luton and Welwyn Garden City from mid-February 1958, then had second thoughts. A withdrawal in mid-school term would create problems reimbursing Local Authority school term tickets, so the withdrawal would be deferred until Easter 1958, and the company was then persuaded to retain the Luton-Kimpton section, which, with one-man operation, could probably be amended to operate profitably. From April 1958, only the Luton to Kimpton section of Birch route 205 continued to operate, with no Sunday service. John Birch suggested to London Transport a Monday to Friday peak hour timetable for a new replacement route between Welwyn Garden City and Kimpton, with no off-peak or Saturday service and worked by RT double-decks, which was largely adopted as their new route 315. From the same date, a number of Birch drivers at Henlow Camp garage agreed to voluntary one-man duties on selected country routes, including the reduced route 205. Conductors were still carried on routes where the drivers hadn't volunteered for the one-person-operation.

During the 1950s, London Transport Country Buses officially split route 321 between Luton & Uxbridge to operate as route 321 (Luton-Maple Cross) and route 351 (Harpenden or St Albans-Uxbridge). For a while, route 351 was diverted at its north-eastern end to operate to Welwyn Garden City instead of Harpenden. Eventually, route 351 was replaced by a new limited stop service numbered 803 (Uxbridge-Welwyn Garden City) operating Monday to Friday peaks and all day Saturday, the latter operation was withdrawn during the early 1960s, whilst some route 321 journeys were curtailed at Rickmansworth to divert to the newly built Berry Lane Estate as route 321A. During the later years of the 1950s, one-man operation gradually spread across the single-deck operated routes of London Transport Country Buses, using 41-seat RF-class AEC Regal IV buses. Luton garage became involved with the summer timetable for May 1959, when routes 356 (Luton-Flamstead), 376 (Luton-Kensworth or Whipsnade Zoo) and 364 (Luton-Breachwood Green-Hitchin) were merged into two new routes numbered 364 (Hitchin-Luton-Flamstead) and 364A (Hitchin-Luton-Kensworth or Whipsnade Zoo). On both routes, very few journeys operated throughout, most ending at Luton, but most were now one man operated using RF-class single-decks. Peak-time journeys and the Sunday operation on the 364 continued to be operated by RT-class double-decks. At the same time, the St Albans-Dunstable route 369, on which some peak hour journeys had been extended from St Albans City Centre or City Station to Sandridge Church, was replaced by a substantial extension of the St Albans-Colney Heath route 343, which now operated between Dunstable, St Albans and Brookmans Park Station, this too retaining double-deck RT operation. Finally, the weekday peak hour journeys operated as route 376A between Studham and Dunstable became route 343A. It was operated by one-man RFs from Luton garage. By the late 1950s, route 352 (Dunstable-Berkhamsted) had been heavily curtailed, operating only on 4 days per week, with the through service only operating on Saturdays, restricted to Dunstable-Dagnall otherwise. The Saturday operation remained single-deck but carried a conductor as it was one of the last regular workings of a T-class AEC Regal III, these being operated from Tring.

The Green Line network had seen a heavy growth in passenger numbers during the mid-1950s, only to see a sharp decline towards the end of the decade, a result of the growth of private motor-car ownership coupled with the conversion of many suburban rail services to diesel traction. Route 726 to Whipsnade Zoo was probably one of the first to show the effect, as levels of duplication required diminished. From the summer timetable for 1957 one of the Romford journeys each way was extended to start from Harold Hill Estate in an attempt to generate more trade; although this remained in the timetable for four years, it was not a success and the Harold Hill journey disappeared after the summer 1960 timetable. In November 1960, route 712 was diverted south of St Albans to serve Chiswell Green and Park Street, the first time routes 712 and 713 had followed different routes south of St Albans. From this time, the frequency of route 712 journeys through to Luton was gradually reduced, with an increasing number of journeys ending at St Albans.

In 1960, the short Luton-Caddington route 360, which remained RT operated, was extended in Caddington from The Green to new housing development at Ledwell Road. Its frequency had been progressively improved during the 1950s, and it was now a frequent and regular service.

The diminishing trade on most Green Line routes was recognised by London Transport from summer 1963. Route 726 was reduced, including its complete withdrawal on Summer Saturdays, with journeys to Whipsnade Zoo being introduced on Saturday & Sunday on route 712 instead, these being designated route 712A, worked from St Albans. Subsequently, some route 713 journeys were cut back from Dunstable to terminate at St Albans instead; eventually, the route followed south of St Albans, rather than its eventual destination, decreed whether a journey was 712 or 713, after six months in which journeys operated as routes 712, 712A, 712B, 713 and 713A. From May 1964, route 726 was diverted to operate non-stop on the section of route between Whipsnade Zoo and Golders Green via the M1 motorway, instead of serving St Albans and Barnet. Although a belated recognition of the existence of the motorway, it brought open-platform RT vehicles on to regular (summer) operation on a motorway, a practice since banned. This was alleviated in summer 1965 when new RCL-class AEC Routemasters with electric platform doors replaced the RT vehicles at Romford, and hence took over route 726. About the same time, the Country Bus route 313 journeys (Enfield-St Albans-Whipsnade Zoo) which were extended in the summer from St Albans to Whipsnade Zoo were largely revised to operate non-stop over the section between St Albans and Whipsnade Zoo.

Birch Bros. Ltd's remaining bus operation in the area of study, route 205 between Luton and Kimpton, was withdrawn after 31 October 1965. Despite the implementation of one-man operation, it had continued to operate at a loss, in the hope of government initiative for a rural bus grant scheme, which was not forthcoming at this time. The route remained unserved for several years but was to see a surprising resurrection from 1968.

Two new routes appeared in the mid-1960s following the closure to passenger traffic on the railway line between Welwyn Garden City and Dunstable, this taking place in April 1965. The Luton to Dunstable section of the route was still open for freight trains at this time. London Transport introduced a new Monday to Saturday service numbered 366, operating between Luton and Welwyn Garden City Station, running via Newmill End, Batford and Wheathampstead. The schedule was made to be limited stop, calling only at stops near the former railway stations; this is believed to be due to Union pressure over the proposed schedules, which were considered too tight for a more conventional one-man operated bus service. In the ensuing years, more and more intermediate stops, or sections of route along which the bus would stop at any safe place, were gradually added. Two additional RF single-deck buses were added to Luton's allocation to work route 366, which created a capacity problem at the garage. London Transport agreed with Luton Borough Council to turn three parking meter bays in Park Street West into a bus parking bay for overnight parking of the last Green Line 714 home, due at 01.15 each night, and also for daytime parking of 714 vehicles from Dorking garage during their one-hour meal relief at Luton, to avoid being blocked in inside the very congested garage.

The second new route was a remarkable innovation for the ailing Green Line network. The idea of orbital routes circumventing the Central London built-up area had been floated back in 1946 with proposed route 719 which was not implemented, but eventually followed up from 1953 with route 725, and route 724 from July 1966, the latter also being the first Green Line route to be one-man operated. Now, the new proposal would link three airports and two main line railway stations as well as serving as an orbital route to the west of London. It was intended as a 'Greenline Express' service, very limited stop, between Luton Airport, Luton Railway Station, St Albans, Watford Junction Station, Uxbridge, Heathrow Airport, Kingston, Gatwick Airport and Crawley, as new route 727. Through railway tickets would be accepted from railway stations on the Midland and West Coast main line to any of the three airports, and vice versa, and the vehicles employed, modified RF-class AEC Regal IV, which by this time were sixteen years old. They gained additional luggage accommodation as a result. The first obstacle was that both Luton Airport and Luton Railway Station were outside the designated London Transport operating area; as a compromise, Luton Airport was dropped and the northern terminus was fixed at Luton Railway Station, still just beyond the London Transport operating area but that would now be ignored. Luton and District, a co-ordination of services between Luton Corporation and United Counties, which has been referred to in the United Counties section of this book, were required to arrange diversion of their local services to and from Luton Airport to provide a direct local bus link between Luton Airport and Luton Railway Station. Route 727 was one-man operated from St Albans and Reigate garages using modified RF-class vehicles, which had their seating capacity reduced to 35 passengers for extra luggage accommodation, high ratio back axles and extra-large fuel tanks made at Aldenham works, leaking badly along the joins, and commenced on 13 May 1967. It was an immediate, enormous success, especially with medium-distance passengers travelling between the towns it served, however this was not quite the intention. The elderly RF-class vehicles were partly replaced by 4-year-old RC-class AEC Reliance coaches, seating 45 passengers, reduced from 49 due to the additional luggage accommodation, by 1969. Although they were much newer vehicles, they soon proved troublesome and sluggish compared with the RFs. In addition, the roads traversed, in the era before the M25, were increasingly congested and poor timekeeping became an unfortunate feature of the service.

Shifting our focus back to London Transport Country Buses, route 360 (Luton-Caddington) was extended further within Caddington in 1963, providing a loop working at Ledwell Road, eliminating the former reverse. At the same time, several afternoon journeys on four days per week were extended from Caddington to Dunstable, still worked by RT-class double-decks with conductors. The latter were made at the cost of some mid-afternoon journeys between Luton and Caddington. The popularity of Dunstable as an alternative shopping centre to Luton, following the completion of The Quadrant in the early 1960s, also led to the introduction of off-peak journeys on three days per week between Kensworth and Dunstable on route 343A, formerly a peak hour service. These journeys were worked by an RF from Hemel Hempstead during layovers between journeys on route 337. On Wednesday and Friday, the most popular shopping days, the vehicle worked the Dunstable-Dagnall journeys on route 352 at these times. On route 352, however, the Sunday service had ended in the 1950s, and the Saturday service was curtailed between Dunstable and Dagnall only by 1963.

One-man operation came to the Watling Street route from Dunstable in the mid-60s when route 343 was cut back to operate mainly between St Albans and Colney Heath, retaining double-deck RT operation, and new single-deck RF route 342 was introduced between St Albans City Station and Dunstable. At peak times, some 343 journeys extended from St Albans to Redbourn, Friars Wash, Flamstead and Markyate, also from Colney Heath to Brookmans Park Station. During the later 1960s, route 321 journeys terminating at Maple Cross, which included much of the service to and from Luton, were extended to serve the new development at Longcroft Road. About the same time, however, route 321A (Luton-Rickmansworth, Berry Lane Estate) was withdrawn, as the estate was also now served, more frequently, by Watford local services.

At the beginning of September 1968, Green Line route 726 was suspended for the winter, being withdrawn permanently a few weeks later. One-man operation, combined with substantially reduced schedules, came to Green Line Route 714 (Dorking-Kingston-London-Barnet-Luton) from November 1968, and Green Line Routes 712 and 713 (Dorking-Epsom-London-Mill Hill-St Albans; journeys to Dunstable, Luton or Whipsnade Zoo) from February 1969. In the latter case, the service to Dunstable was now reduced to Monday to Friday peak hour journeys only, and to Luton to just two journeys per weekday, although the summer timetable gave a slightly increased daily service to Whipsnade Zoo due to the withdrawal of route 726.

A bus link was re-established between Luton and Kimpton in September 1968, the route being abandoned by Birch Bros. in October 1965. The new service initially operated once a week. The Association of Public Transport Users, a voluntary group but much inspired by their publicity-conscious Secretary, George Ausden of Ampthill, obtained a licence to operate a service between Codicote and Luton, via Kimpton and Peters Green on Friday mornings, initially using coaches hired from Stevenage Travel Ltd. The latter company ran into financial problems in early 1969, and the operation of the APTU service passed to Blatchley's 'Contract Us', of Stevenage, using a second-hand double-deck Bristol K5G. This was only possible because of the removal of a very low railway bridge over the B653 at Newmill End at the time, redundant since the closure of the Hatfield-Luton railway link. The service continued into 1970, when further changes were implemented.

The implementation of the Transport (London) Act 1969 from 1 January 1970 entrusted the London Underground network and London Transport Central Buses to the Greater London Council as a new London Transport Executive. London Transport Country Buses and Coaches passed to the state-owned National Bus Company (NBC) as London Country Bus Services Ltd. From this date routes that entered the area concerned in this chapter at the time of takeover were as follows:

313 Enfield-St Albans-Whipsnade Zoo (Summers only)
321 Luton-Uxbridge (most journeys terminating at Maple Cross from Luton)
337 Dunstable-Boxmoor

342 Dunstable-St Albans
343 Markyate (peaks)-St Albans-Colney Heath/Brookmans Park
343A Dunstable-Studham
352 Dunstable-Dagnall
360 Luton-Caddington (journeys to Dunstable)
364 Hitchin-Breachwood Green-Luton-Flamstead
364A Hitchin-Breachwood Green-Luton-Kensworth-Whipsnade Zoo (summer)
365 Luton-Wheathampstead-St Albans (Sat & Sun only)
366 Luton-Wheathampstead-Welwyn Garden City

Green Line

712/713 Luton-Dunstable/Whipsnade Zoo-St Albans-Mill Hill-London-Epsom-Dorking
714 Luton-Barnet-London-Kingston-Dorking
727 Luton Station-Luton-St Albans-Watford-Heathrow-Kingston-Gatwick-Crawley

The new Company's management criticised the age of the vehicles it had acquired, the lack of progress towards one-man operation on the longer bus routes, and the cost of providing the network of village bus services acquired. These were ominous omens for the immediate future. An early bonus, however, was the extension of Green Line route 727 to Luton Airport in March 1971, the NBC having assumed responsibility for local bus services in the Luton Area with the acquisition of Luton Corporation Transport on 4 January 1970. By 1971, route 727 was entirely operated by RC-class AEC Reliance coaches, but these were soon superseded by new RP-class AEC Reliances.

Meanwhile, the APTU service between Luton, Kimpton and Codicote had further changes. Blatchley's Contract Us was replaced as operator by Chisholm of Wheathampstead. He was foremost a road haulier but had a Ford Transit minibus for hire. The service was revised to operate between Luton and Kimpton only, but now ran several times each day, on Fridays and Saturdays. The timetable was again altered to include several journeys serving the hamlet of Copt Hall, located between Chiltern Green and Luton, which had never before (or since) been served by public transport, the narrow access roads precluding anything larger than a Ford Transit. An extension in Luton to and from the Luton Town Football Ground was even advertised on two Saturday afternoon journeys on the occasion of home matches. The stage carriage licence was still held by George Ausden but now trading as 'Action for Passenger Transport'. At some time during 1971, the hire of Chisholm's minibus ceased, and operation reverted to a full-sized coach hired from Jey-Son Coaches, of Luton. The timetable was revised and slightly reduced, excluding the Copt Hall and Luton Football Ground diversions, but the Saturday timetable now included two journeys extended from Kimpton to and from Codicote. At some stage, it was agreed that Hertfordshire County Council would pay a Rural Bus Grant to either George Ausden or Jey-Son for the maintenance of this service.

The Studham-Kensworth-Dunstable peak hour and shoppers' journeys were renumbered during 1971 from 343A to be part of route 364A, whilst the Saturday & Sunday only route 365 between St Albans and Luton via Wheathampstead was withdrawn. London Country sought local council grant aid to support its village bus services during 1971. The request was initially received relatively favourably in Hertfordshire and Surrey, both quite wealthy county authorities, but Bedfordshire had no budget allowance, and delegated the problem to the district councils, who had neither budget allowance nor actual cash. The same stance was taken in Buckinghamshire, responsible for Dagnall. London Country stood their ground with demands for subsidies for routes 337, 352, 364, and 364A, although 337 and 364 both operated partly in Hertfordshire, who were to pay subsidies. Routes 352 and 364A were withdrawn, although the Luton to Hitchin journeys on the 364A were transferred to route 364. Route 337 was withdrawn between Studham and Dunstable. Route 364, however, would continue to operate between Hitchin, Breachwood Green, Luton, Markyate and Flamstead, but would no longer operate via Woodside, or stop at Slip End, both places within Luton Rural District Council's area. The latter restraint was reversed by the Traffic Commissioner, but only for passengers travelling between Slip End and Markyate; the doctors' surgery covering Slip End was located in Markyate. The implementation would take effect from 19 February 1972.

Weekday replacements for the service were to be operated by Cook's Coaches of Dunstable, centred on Dunstable rather than Luton, with a Monday to Saturday service between Dunstable and Studham via Kensworth, the route followed by the former 364A works journeys, a Monday to Friday peak-time service between Luton, Slip End, Woodside, Kensworth and Whipsnade Zoo, and a Wednesday and Sunday only service between Dunstable and Dagnall.

A new replacement service for Slip End and Woodside was proposed by R.A. Keech, trading as Hillside Coaches. The proprietor of this firm, Ronald Keech, was a resident of Slip End. The proposal was for the service to be a Monday to Saturday service between Luton and Dunstable, serving Slip End, Woodside, Aley Green and Mancroft Road, Caddington, providing a new all-day link between Dunstable and Slip End, Woodside and Caddington. Hillside Coaches themselves were expanding at this time due to their involvement with charter holiday traffic operated by the Court Line Group. At the end of 1971, Hillside Coaches were incorporated into the Court Line Group as Court Line Coaches Ltd. At the same time discussions were opened with Cook's Coaches regarding the acquisition of this company.

The new bus services were introduced under the Court Line Coaches title from 19 February, although the acquisition of Cook's Coaches was not completed until May 1972. The new services were numbered 1 Dunstable-Studham; 2 Luton-Whipsnade Zoo; 3 Luton-Slip End-Dunstable and 4 Dunstable-Dagnall; the service number 5 was also allocated to an existing market day express service linking Pitstone with Leighton Buzzard on Tuesday and Saturday, which Cook's Coaches had operated for several years. Residents of Mancroft Road, Caddington successfully objected to the operation of a regular bus service along their road, which they considered too narrow, so service 3 was diverted via Little Green Lane, Manor Road and Caddington Green, traversing an even narrower road, Little Green Lane, and bringing the route into direct competition with London Country route 360. Bus grant specification Plaxton-bodied 45-seat Ford coaches were ordered for the new services, in a pastel green livery, but only one was available for service for the initial months, with ex-Hillside Coaches vehicles making up the shortfall. One similar new 45-seat Ford was also delivered to Cook's Coaches in their purple and white livery; although subsequently adorned with a Court Line fleet name, it retained the Cook's Coaches livery throughout its life on Court Line bus work.

A strange anomaly within London Country operations in the area was created by these changes, in that the Sunday service between Luton and Markyate on route 364 continued to operate, virtually non-stop between its two destinations, as most of this section of route was within Bedfordshire but remained worked by double-deck

RT vehicles with conductors, as no one-man duties were scheduled from Luton on a Sunday. Meanwhile, there were developments on the Dunstable-St Albans road. During the summer of 1971, one-man operation was substantially increased at St Albans garage, mostly using AEC Swifts acquired, almost brand new, from South Wales Transport. Route 343 was one route affected, and it was linked to the erstwhile 342 (Dunstable-St Albans) again to provide a through service between Dunstable and Welham Green or Colney Heath as route 343. The number 342 did not remain vacant for long as it was reused for Saturday journeys which operated between Dunstable, St Albans and London Colney. A victim of these changes was Saturday & Sunday route 365 (St Albans-Wheathampstead-Luton) which ceased to operate. Some Monday to Friday peak hour journeys had briefly appeared on the route between Luton, Vauxhall Works and Batford Mill, but these had also disappeared.

On 16 July 1972, one-man operation came to route 321, when new AN-class Leyland Atlanteans were introduced to the route. The Dunstable journeys on route 360 were also transferred to the one-man rota, but using RF-class single-decks, leaving just 2 RTs at Luton to work the Luton-Caddington section of route 360. The Sunday route 364 journeys between Luton and Markyate were withdrawn at the same time. The apparent success of the country bus services introduced by Court Line Coaches in February 1972 encouraged Hertfordshire County Council to review its bus grant policy and they would no longer support route 364 or the Boxmoor to Studham section of route 337 when grants were reviewed in July 1973. Court Line Coaches introduced a new route 6 between Luton Airport, Luton, Slip End, Woodside, Markyate and Flamstead, whilst the existing service 1 (Dunstable-Studham) was extended through to Hemel Hempstead. The Luton to Hitchin section of route 364 was taken over from the following Monday by Jey-son Coaches of Luton, after London Country had operated a special timetable on route 364 between Luton and Hitchin only on the final Saturday, with Court Line having already taken over the Luton-Flamstead section. In fact, the Court Line changes were part of a revised timetable for all their bus services, incorporating more regular frequencies. They never operated on Sunday, but now offered a Bank Holiday service on their main services.

The next round of major service revisions took place in June 1974. This would involve a regular daytime interchange, every two hours, at the rural outpost of Gaddesden Row, where three buses would meet and interchange some through passengers. Services 6 and 7 were now designated through services between Luton and Hemel Hempstead, service 6 via Markyate, Flamstead and the M1 Motorway, service 7 via Markyate and Gaddesden Row. There were now 8 pastel green liveried Plaxton-bodied Fords in the bus fleet, whilst the coach fleet now exceeded 60 vehicles, almost all Plaxton-bodied Fords less than 3 years old. The majority of the coaches was employed on airport feeder work for Court Line's package holiday customers, although some school contract work and extended tours work was also carried out. During the week in June 1974 prior to implementation of the new bus timetable, it was announced that trading in shares in Court Line plc, the parent group, had ceased on the Stock Exchange. Debts incurred by Clarkson's, the former package holiday business, had proven far greater than anticipated, and Stock Market confidence in Court Line plc had vanished. But day-to-day business continued as usual for another two months, and the increased bus timetable was introduced.

On a Thursday evening in mid-August 1974, Court Line plc was plunged into Receivership. Exceptionally, Court Line Coaches Ltd. continued to trade, but with much of its coach fleet reliant on Court Line's package holiday customers, there was suddenly little business apart from the bus work. Although schools were on holiday, Court Line Coaches Ltd. had already gained contracts for the new autumn term, which the local authorities concerned were now viewing with alarm. The bus operations continued, but almost all coach drivers and maintenance staff were immediately laid off. In the ensuing months, maintenance problems with any of the eight designated buses were covered by taking one of the accessible serviceable coaches from the multitude parked in the yard at the Luton Airport premises. By December 1974, only four of the eight bus fleet vehicles were reputedly serviceable. Tricentrol Coaches Ltd. had shown interest in buying the coach fleet from the Receiver, but only if any commitment to continue the bus work was not included, something the Receiver would not agree. The acquisition of Court Line Coaches by United Counties has already been covered under that section, but for completeness it is mentioned here as well. United Counties at the time were beset with accommodation problems in Luton as building work on extending Castle Street garage was behind schedule. The Receiver gave notice that Court Line Coaches Ltd's remaining operations, the bus work, would cease at the end of the first week of December 1974, just as Christmas shopping reached its peak. The final day saw a round of meetings involving two County Council Transport Co-ordinators, various management staff from the National Bus Company and United Counties, and even London Country, Luton Airport Management, as landlords for the premises, and other officers from Luton Corporation. Eventually, it was agreed that United Counties would acquire the eight bus fleet vehicles and operate the services from the following Monday morning. Initially, the operating base would remain at Luton Airport until temporary accommodation could be placed on the forecourt of Luton Corporation's Kingsway garage, the former bus garage at this point was being used as a municipal refuse depot and Post Office Telephones vehicle depot, for use by United Counties. United Counties would offer employment to the remaining Court Line drivers, most of whom had formerly been United Counties drivers. Four withdrawn Bristol LS5G buses would be temporarily returned to service without recertification until the ex-Court Line Fords were all serviceable. In the event, the LS5G buses proved very temperamental and only added to the problems of the following weeks, with only two of the four still serviceable after the three-week period.

In February 1975, the former Court Line services were renumbered to 40 (Luton-Slip End-Caddington-Dunstable), 41 (Dunstable-Gaddesden Row-Hemel Hempstead), 42 (Luton-Whipsnade Zoo), 44 (Dunstable-Dagnall), 46 (Luton-Markyate-Flamstead-M1-Hemel Hempstead) and 47 (Luton-Markyate-Gaddesden Row-Hemel Hempstead).

In the summer of 1975, Jey-Son Coaches announced their intention of giving up their bus services, although the licence for the Luton-Kimpton-Codicote service was actually still held by George Ausden. It was agreed that the Luton-Breachwood Green-Hitchin service would pass to United Counties in July 1975, initially as their service 81, but renumbered 88 when operation was transferred from Luton to Hitchin during the following year. The replacement for the Luton-Kimpton-Codicote service, however, was, rather surprisingly, having spent so many years divesting their country bus services in the area, operated by London Country from Luton garage, who allocated the service number 365 to the route. It lasted less than 18 months, for the long-predicted closure of London Country's Luton Garage was announced to take effect at the end of January 1977. In the meantime, the Luton terminus at Park Square, used by most London Country services, had been transferred to the new Bute

Street Bus Station during September 1976, where several so-called 'drive-through' bays had been added for their use, at the back of the vehicle circulating area, to supplement the 'nose in, reverse out' arrangement used for United Counties' services. London Country drivers refused to reverse buses on service unless operating with a conductor.

December 1976 saw United Counties take over operation of the Luton to Caddington section of London Country route 360, as their service 6, the Dunstable journeys on route 360 being withdrawn as they were more than adequately covered by United Counties' service 40, the former Court Line operation. United Counties' service 6 continued to be operated with conductors, but on single-deck Bristol RELL buses, for the time being. The last RT operation by London Country at Luton had actually taken place earlier in the summer, as route 360 had been operated by AN-class Leyland Atlanteans, albeit with conductors, during its final months of operation. At the same time, route 365 (Luton-Kimpton-Codicote) became United Counties' service 45.

London Country closed Luton garage at the end of January 1977, when Garston took over complete operation of route 321 (Luton-Uxbridge), having previously provided the majority share of the routes' duties. Green Line route 714 (Luton-Dorking) was finally withdrawn between Luton and London, this section being replaced by two new Green Line limited stop routes, 707 (Luton Airport-Luton-St Albans-Barnet-Golders Green-Victoria) and 717 (Luton Airport-Luton-St Albans-Borehamwood-Brent Cross-Victoria), both operated by St Albans (SA) using new RS-class Plaxton coach-bodied AEC Reliances. The new routes also replaced the remaining section of Green Line routes 712 and 713 between St Albans and Victoria, which were also withdrawn at this time. Green Line route 727 (Luton Airport-Heathrow-Gatwick-Crawley) was already worked by St Albans (SA) and Reigate (RG) garages and continued unchanged.

The subsequent summer 1977 timetable for Green Line brought the introduction of a further new limited stop route 737 between Victoria and Whipsnade Zoo via Golders Green and the M1 motorway to replace the former 713 journeys to Whipsnade Zoo in summer only. It was later extended from Whipsnade Zoo to Woburn at weekends, offering very reasonably priced day trips from anywhere on the Green Line network to either Whipsnade Zoo or Woburn for the price of London Country's then recently-introduced 'Golden Rover' ticket. Unfortunately, lack of publicity did not do it justice, and route 737 was usually poorly patronised. United Counties' new service to Caddington was quickly incorporated into the Luton town service network, as service 6 was extended from Luton Bus Station to Warden Hill Road and converted to one-man operation, replacing former service 26. Later, the Friday and Saturday service 45 (Luton-Kimpton-Codicote) was replaced by a new Monday to Saturday service 44 operating through between Luton and Stevenage, via Kimpton and Codicote, making use of new roads through a recent housing development between Codicote and Stevenage. This brought London Country back onto the scene, as the new service was jointly worked by United Counties from Luton, and London Country from their Stevenage garage (SV) for a short period of time.

The final London Country service to operate into Luton was the 321, operating between the town and St Albans, Watford and Rickmansworth. Operated from Garston, it continued to be operated by London Country Bus Services and its successor, London Country North West, until this company was purchased by Luton & District in 1990.

The Union Jack (Luton) Omnibus Co. Ltd. was one of a number of operations owned by A.F. England, operating in Bedfordshire. They operated a varied fleet of buses including this Dennis E saloon registered YU1018. The vehicle took up fleet number 21 in the Union Jack fleet. *D.W.K. Jones Archive/S.J. Butler Collection*

Luton finds
London Transport T382 (PL6458), a Weymann bodied AEC Regal. It is seen about to embark on a journey on the 356A to Flamstead. The T-class were used to replace some of the former Strawhatter Gilford coaches. *D.W.K. Jones Archive/ S.J. Butler Collection*

The fleet of Gilford coaches operated by Strawhatter coaches were added to the GF-class when acquired by London Transport on 1 February 1934. GF163 (MJ75), a Gilford 168OT, is seen in Harpenden in July 1934 whilst operating service 51 to Luton.
D.W.K. Jones Archive/ S.J. Butler Collection

Dunstable Market Square finds RT3051 (KXW160) operating a journey on the 360 to Luton. The main route operated between Luton and Caddington, with certain journeys being extended out to Dunstable.
S.J. Butler Collection

Route 321 still operates today, albeit a shorter version of the original route. The main type for the route in the 1960s was the AEC Regent. Weymann bodied RT3129 (KXW238) is seen negotiating Castle Street, Luton in this April 1966 view whilst heading towards Maple Cross. *Graham Smith*

RT3253 (LLU612) is seen operating a journey on Green Line route 713 in September 1968. It is seen passing the Caddington Turn on Watling Street. This Weymann bodied AEC Regent was new to London Transport in July 1950. *Graham Smith*

London Transport operated a number of AEC Regents in the Luton area. Weymann bodied RT4041 (LUC200) is seen operating a journey on route 360 towards Luton. It is seen travelling along Dunstable Road in the scenic village of Caddington. *Graham Smith*

Market Hill, Luton finds London Transport's RF42 (LYF402). It is seen operating route 364 bound for Tea Green. The route originated with London General as their N64 service, being operated by the National Omnibus Company on their behalf. *Graham Smith*

On 13 May 1967 a new Green Line service, the 727, commenced operation, becoming the first London Transport route to use Luton Railway Station as a terminus. It is at this location that we find RF138 (MLL525), the vehicle used on the first journey of this service. *Graham Smith*

In its heyday, the 352 operated between Dunstable and Berkhamsted. However, by 1963 the route had been curtailed to operate between Dunstable and Dagnall, running on a Saturday only. Dunstable, Market Square finds RF578 (NLE578). *S.J. Butler Collection*

In **1965** London Transport replaced a fleet of RT-class Regents on Green Line service 726 between London and Dunstable/ Whipsnade Zoo with a new fleet of AEC Routemaster coaches, becoming the RCL-class. RCL2224 (CUV224C) is seen at Kensworth, Packhorse heading back to Romford via Central London. The 726 was operated out from the Country area garage in Romford. *Graham Smith*

A far cry from the coaching operation of today on the Green Line service 757. Luton Airport finds London Country's Leyland National SNB149 (HPF299N) loading before its journey into London. Note the two airport buses on the left-hand side of this photograph. *Gary Seamarks*

The Leyland National was taken up as one of the standard models of National Bus Company subsidiaries during the 1970s, with London Country being no exception. A fine example, SNC199 (UPE199M), is seen at Park Square, Luton before departing on a journey on route 360 to Dunstable. This service was taken over by United Counties in 1976. *Graham Smith*

Green Line service 727 ran from Crawley to Luton Airport, via Gatwick Airport, Heathrow Airport, Uxbridge and parts of Hertfordshire. Seen passing the Arndale Shopping Centre in Church Street is Crawley based AEC Reliance RP46 (JPA146K) sporting an all-over advertisement for fast food chain Wimpy. The route travelled through the town centre to reach Luton Airport. *Graham Smith*

The new order in the early 1970s called for a large number of Leyland Atlanteans to replace the older rolling stock inherited from London Transport. July 1975 finds a pair of London Country vehicles passing through Park Street, Luton. AN50 (JPL150K) is seen leading the pair, whilst completing its journey on route 321. *Graham Smith*

London Country was split into five smaller operations in 1986 in preparation for the sale of the company by the National Bus Company. Garston garage came under the new London Country North West operation. It was from this garage that route 321 operated. Bute Street bus station finds LR53 (A153FPG), normally used on the company's London Regional Transport contracts in the Edgware and Harrow areas of north London, shown by the sticker on the front near side of the vehicle. *Gary Seamarks*

BTL2 (B102KPF), a Berkhof bodied Leyland Tiger, is seen here entering Bute Street bus station on the new 'Jetlink' express service linking Gatwick, Heathrow and Luton Airports. The service was later operated by the newly formed Speedlink Airport Services company, with a revised livery being carried by vehicles. The 'Jetlink' brand expanded, with routes in the heyday operating to Norwich, Northampton and Brighton. *Gary Seamarks*

The late 1990s saw six Plaxton Prestige bodied DAF SB220 saloons purchased by The Shires to operate route 321 (Rickmansworth-Luton), supported by a fleet of similar vehicles acquired from Arriva Scotland West. 3275 (V275HBH) was one of the new vehicles and is seen carrying route branding of the service. However, it is seen here being used on Watford town route 10. *Liam Farrer-Beddall*

The last dedicated batch of vehicles to be purchased for the 321 were ten Wrightbus Streetlite DF saloons, delivered to Arriva the Shires in July 2014. These saloons were built to Sapphire specification and wore Sapphire livery as can be seen above. The penultimate member of the batch, 3659 (LK14FTO), is seen at Luton Interchange, starting its journey south to Watford. *Liam Farrer-Beddall*

CHAPTER FOUR
LUTON GUIDED BUSWAY

The route between Luton and Dunstable had for many years been a slow one, with many wanting a faster, more direct route between the two towns. An early attempt at this was the SuperRider limited stop service introduced by United Counties using a pair of Leyland Nationals. The opening of Hatters Way in the late 1980s saw several services diverted down this new link road, helping to slightly speed up services, but this had limited success.

Further ideas began to be investigated by Bedfordshire County Council as they considered how they could lessen the amount of time taken for people to travel on public transport between Luton and Dunstable from 1989. A number of options were considered including a branch line of the Thameslink rail route already serving the main line through the town. The line would run direct trains between Dunstable and London. However, a number of obstacles stood in the way of these plans. Firstly, the original branch line between Luton and Dunstable had no connection to the Midland main line, the line continued on from Hatfield to King's Cross. The building of Hatters Way narrowed the original track bed, sealing the fate of this idea. The other options were a twin-track light rail system or a guided busway.

The guided busway option was deemed to be the most cost-effective choice and was therefore selected as the preferred option in 1996. Control of the project was taken away from Bedfordshire County Council and handed to the new unitary authority, Luton Borough Council, upon its formation in 1997. The route chosen for the project was the former Dunstable branch line which had been closed to rail traffic since 1967.

Construction began on the Busway in 2010 and took three years to complete. Seven new bridges were constructed, along with three existing ones rebuilt. New specialist bus stops and a transport interchange next to Luton railway station were also included. In total the project cost around £91 million to build.

The 7.7 mile guided section was opened on 24 September 2013, running between Dunstable, Houghton Regis and Luton Interchange. It opened five months after it was originally supposed to have done. An additional section was built, although not guided, between Luton Interchange and Kimpton Road, a road reserved for bus operations only. In addition to Busway services, this section is also used by National Express and Stagecoach East, speeding up journey times between Luton town centre and Luton Airport. The Busway, as at 2020, was served by three operators, Arriva the Shires, Centrebus and Flitwick based Grant Palmer Travel.

Wright Urban bodied Volvo B7RLE 3961 (KX12GZZ) is seen travelling down the busway heading towards Luton Interchange. This view shows the track bed. *Gary Seamarks*

Another view of a Wright Urban bodied Volvo B7RLE saloon owned by Arriva the Shires. 3966 (LT63UNK) is seen having left the Guided Busway, approaching Luton Interchange. *Gary Seamarks*

Grant Palmer operates service C between Luton Interchange and Dunstable town centre. The vehicles used on the service gained private registration plates. Scania OmniCity BU51WAY is seen on its way to Dunstable. *Gary Seamarks*

Centrebus ran two services using the Busway, one to Dunstable, the other to Houghton Regis and Toddington. East Lancs Esteem bodied Scania saloon 706 (K3YCL) was part of the original batch of vehicles used by Centrebus on Busway services. *Gary Seamarks*

CHAPTER FIVE

LUTON & DISTRICT TO ARRIVA THE SHIRES

The National Bus Company made the decision to divide its larger bus operations into smaller units to make them easier to sell. From 1 January 1986 Luton & District Limited took over the former United Counties Omnibus Company garages in Buckingham Street, Aylesbury; Fishponds Road, Hitchin; and Castle Street, Luton. Luton & District took responsibility at this point for these garages, having outstations in Leighton Buzzard and Toddington. The Leighton Buzzard outstation became a garage in its own right in May 1987. The new operator used local identities for its fleet, these being 'Aylesbury Bus', 'Hitchin Bus' and 'Luton Bus', the coaching unit gaining the new fleet name 'Crusader Travel'.

A handful of local independent operators were acquired by Luton & District over its history. The first took place on 30 January 1988, the first of two to be acquired during that year. On this date, the business of Red Rover Omnibus Limited, Aylesbury was taken over. This added a second operating base in Aylesbury, located on Bicester Road. In June, the services and vehicles operated by Milton Keynes Coaches Limited (Tourmaster) of Dunstable were acquired. Again, this added another operating base, this time located in Tavistock Street, Dunstable. This was originally an outstation of Luton, gaining full garage status on 16 October 1988. The Dunstable Bus fleet name was used. It was on this date that the outstation in Toddington, dating back to the days of Road Motors Ltd in the 1920s, was closed, Dunstable replacing it.

The full-garage status of Leighton Buzzard did not last long. In early August 1988, Luton & District opened a new outstation at Avery's Garage located in Plantation Road, Leighton Buzzard. This replaced the company's premises at North Street. Routes 69 and 70 to Luton were transferred to Dunstable at this time.

Two significant takeovers took place during 1990. The first happened on 20 May when a large percentage of the Sovereign Bus & Coach Ltd operation in Stevenage was acquired. The acquisition brought forty-two vehicles with it, along with a garage at Danestreet, Stevenage. Both Luton & District and Sovereign shared this site for a while.

The largest acquisition took place on 12 October 1990 when the operations and vehicles of London Country Bus (North West) Limited, Garston were acquired. This acquisition almost doubled the size of the Luton & District fleet and added six new operating bases. These were at The Broadway, Amersham; St Albans Road, Garston; West Wycombe Road, High Wycombe; and Stoke Road, Slough. The final two were located in Hemel Hempstead, where two garages were located, one at Whiteleaf Road, the other at Two Waters. As with the original Luton & District operation, local identities were used. The Amersham and High Wycombe area used the 'Chiltern Bus' name; Garston originally used the name 'Watford Bus', later 'Watfordwide'. 'Hemel Bus' and 'Slough Bus' were also used for the relevant garages. The Lee and District operation was also included in this sale, which operated from the Amersham base. The acquisition of London Country North West divided Luton & District into two operating divisions. The first focused on Bedfordshire, Berkshire and Buckinghamshire; the second solely focused on Hertfordshire. The former fleet numbers applied to the London Country North West fleet pre-take over were retained for a number of years, with any new vehicles being numbered into that series, which used letter prefixes.

28 May 1991 saw the former Red Rover Limited garage in Aylesbury replaced by a new facility in Brunel Road. Later in the year a new garage was opened in Norton Green Road, Stevenage. This replaced the former London Country premises in Danestreet, taking effect from 3 August.

Further new garage facilities were opened in 1992, this time in Buckinghamshire. On 22 March, a new garage was opened on the Cressex Industrial Estate in High Wycombe, located on Lincoln Road. This again led to the closure of the original West Wycombe Road garage in the town. A month later, the garage in Amersham was closed, the Lee and District operation transferring ... to Slough, whilst the bus operation transferred to High Wycombe. December 1992 saw a new outstation established in a public car park in Chesham, but due to local objections it closed after a week of operation.

Luton & District inherited a garage in Slough from London Country (North West) in 1990, this being more remote from the main area of operation. In February 1993 Slough was sold, along with the vehicles and routes, to Q Drive Buses Limited of Wokingham, trading in that area as the Bee Line.

British Bus plc acquired the business of Luton & District in June 1994. The first acquisition under this new owner took place on 1 October. On this date, the business of Stuart Palmer of Dunstable, one of Luton & District's competitors in the Luton and Dunstable area, was purchased. A number of vehicles were acquired along with a garage in Southwood Road, Dunstable. This latter premises was retained solely to operate the former Stuart Palmer services.

Luton & District was relaunched in June 1995, with a new fleet name, new local identities and a new livery being introduced. The new livery was of blue and yellow, with a mushroom-coloured skirt, replacing the red and cream and silver and green liveries worn by the fleet. The new local identities were Aylesbury & the Vale; Chiltern Rover; Elstree & Borehamwood; Gade Valley; Hitchin & District; Luton & Dunstable; network Watford and the Stevenage Line.

Just before the relaunch, the first of two independents to be acquired in 1995 was taken over. In May, the bus services and a number of vehicles of Buffalo Travel of Flitwick, Bedfordshire were acquired, the operator retaining its coaching fleet, along with school contracts. The second operator to be acquired was Motts of Stoke Mandeville. Like Buffalo, not all of the operation was taken over, with just the principal bus services and a small number of vehicles being taken over.

March 1996 saw the former Stuart Palmer garage in Dunstable close. The only other significant event to note for 1996 was the acquisition of British Bus plc by the Cowie Group plc, this taking place on 1 August.

1997 commenced with another acquisition of a local independent operator. On 8 January, the bus and coach operation of Watford based Lucketts were acquired, along with seventeen vehicles. This added a garage at Tolpits Lane, Watford. The Lucketts of Watford fleet name was retained, although vehicles were repainted into the yellow and blue livery. A second independent was swallowed up by The Shires on 24 April 1997, Checkers Cars of Pinner, Middlesex, which was already based at Garston, and was operated as a separate private hire unit.

It has been mentioned above that the original Luton & District operation and former London Country (North West) fleets were operating using two separate fleet numbering systems. On 1 March 1997 the fleet was renumbered into a four-digit series, replacing both series. This made the transfer of vehicles between garages much easier.

The last thing to note for 1997 was that, on 14 October, the Cowie Group relaunched itself as Arriva, this incorporating the British Bus brand too. A new livery was introduced with this, replacing the yellow and blue. A livery of turquoise and cream was used, with local fleet names also disappearing. The Shires altered its name to Arriva the Shires.

14 March 1998 saw the operations of Luton based independent operator Lutonian Buses acquired by Arriva the Shires. This added a new garage in Sedgewick Road, Leagrave, with a number of minibuses being added to the fleet. 1998 also saw the Arriva group restructure its operations in London and the Home Counties. At this time, Arriva the Shires became responsible for several other operations, these being Arriva East Herts & Essex, Arriva Colchester and Arriva Southend. The East Herts & Essex operation added garages in Harlow, Ware and Grays, with an outstation in Debden, Essex (this being an outstation of Harlow). 1 January 1999 saw the East Herts & Essex fleet renumbered into a unified numbering system with the main Arriva the Shires fleet.

After a ruling by the Monopolies and Mergers Commission, it was decided that the Lutonian Buses fleet, acquired by Arriva the Shires in 1998, should be sold. The sale took place on 22 September when it was sold to a private group.

The operation in the High Wycombe area was expanded from 13 December 2000 when Arriva purchased the operations of the Wycombe Bus Company from the Go-Ahead Group, this operation having been a division of the Oxford Bus Company. Fifty-two buses were acquired with this operation.

A new garage and head office was opened at 487 Dunstable Road, Luton on 23 September 2001. This new facility displaced the former Castle Street, Luton and Dunstable garages. However, Castle Street remained open for a short while as not all the maintenance facilities were ready in time for opening.

Another re-organisation of Arriva's operations in the Home Counties took place from 1 January 2002. From this date Arriva the Shires lost control of Grays, Colchester and Southend garages, these transferring to sister company Arriva Southern Counties' control from this date. This led to the loss of 181 vehicles from The Shires fleet.

On 23 January 2005, the remaining operation of Sovereign Bus & Coach was acquired by Arriva. At this time, forty-eight vehicles were acquired, garaged at premises in Hatfield and Babbage Road, Stevenage. Hatfield at this time was an outstation of Stevenage, closing on 6 August 2005.

Another significant acquisition took place on 13 February 2006. On this date, Arriva plc acquired the operations of MK Metro of Milton Keynes. No less than 115 vehicles were acquired along with garages in the town. Milton Keynes was already within

The Shires network, with a number of routes operating to the town from Aylesbury and Luton. The operation retained its yellow livery for a number of years.

Just under a year later, on 13 January 2007, the former United Counties garage in Hitchin closed its doors for the last time. Operations were transferred to nearby Stevenage after this date.

The Milton Keynes operation had expanded since its acquisition by Arriva in 2006. By 2009, there was a need for a new garage. It was in this year that a new garage was opened in Colts Holms Road, replacing the Arden Park facility. On 7 February 2010, the Bleak Hall garage in Milton Keynes was also closed. It was replaced by a new garage on Old Wolverton Road, along with the Colts Holm Road garage. A couple of months later, the yellow livery of MK Metro was discontinued, with the Arriva corporate livery being adopted by the fleet.

Another Essex garage was lost on 16 August, when the Harlow operations transferred to sister Arriva operator Tellings Golden Miller who used the Network Harlow brand. The routes continued initially to operate on the Arriva East Herts & Essex operators' licence.

1 January 2013 saw the MK Metro operators' licence cease, with the fleet being transferred onto the main Arriva the Shires licence.

1 January 2016 saw another re-organisation of the Arriva operations in London and the Home Counties. From this date, Hemel Hempstead, Stevenage and Ware were transferred to the control of Arriva Southern Counties, leaving Arriva the Shires with garages at Luton, Milton Keynes, Aylesbury and High Wycombe. Control of these garages passed to Arriva Midlands, although the Arriva the Shires operators' licence was retained. From the same date, control of the London routes transferred from The Shires to Arriva London, although vehicles initially remained operating on The Shires operators' licence. The non-London routes at Garston transferred to Hemel Hempstead from this date, with the exception of the 321 which moved north to Luton. Arriva London officially took control of the Garston TfL services from 29 October 2016.

New in January 1968, 311 (NBD311F) was the oldest vehicle taken into stock from United Counties in January 1986. It is seen here wearing the red and ivory livery whilst entering Luton Bus Station in this August 1987 shot. *Gary Seamarks*

Representing the large volume of Bristol VRTs taken into stock from United Counties is 774 (ANV774J). It is seen heading for Runfold whilst operating service 9. The former National Bus Company green livery is seen here, complete with Luton Bus fleet names. *Gary Seamarks*

753 (RRP753G) and 865 (TNH865R) are two examples of the ECW bodied Bristol VRT acquired from United Counties. They are seen displaying two of the new identities worn by Luton & District vehicles. 753 is seen heading back to its home garage of Aylesbury, whilst 865 is seen operating a local Luton service. *Gary Seamarks*

Luton town centre finds 481 (RNV481M), a Leyland National saloon acquired from United Counties in January 1986, and is another vehicle sporting the new livery. Note the National Bus Company liveried Bristol VRT in the background. *Gary Seamarks*

The newest double-decks to be acquired from United Counties were nine ECW bodied Leyland Olympians dating back to 1981. Representing this batch is 614 (ARP614X), seen negotiating Luton town centre whilst heading for Runfold. *Gary Seamarks*

The newest vehicles to be acquired from United Counties were six Carlyle bodied Ford Transit minibuses, new in December 1985. 21 (C21NVV) is seen here wearing the Hoppanstopper livery worn by the company's minibuses. *Gary Seamarks*

May 1986 saw the first new vehicles taken into stock by Luton & District. These were further examples of the Carlyle bodied Ford Transit minibus. They were purchased to operate Leighton Buzzard town services, wearing a dedicated livery, branded 'Buzza'. 29 (C193KBH) is seen here in Leighton Buzzard town centre. *Gary Seamarks*

Thirty-four Freight Rover Sherpa minibuses were purchased by the company during 1987, bodied by either Dormobile or Carlyle. Showing the latter bodywork is 90 (D405SGS), seen showing off the Hoppanstopper livery. *Gary Seamarks*

Eight ECW bodied Bristol VRTs were taken into stock by the company during November 1986 from Lincolnshire Road Car Co. Ltd. 844 (OTO153R) is seen departing Luton town centre, whilst heading for Dunstable on route 38. *Gary Seamarks*

Duple bodied Leyland Tiger B500TCJ (108) was acquired by Luton & District from Cheltenham & Gloucester in September 1987. *Gary Seamarks*

January 1988 saw the acquisition of the business of Red Rover Omnibus, Aylesbury. With it came a number of older double-deckers, including MLK419L, a former London Transport Leyland Fleetline. *D.J. Hancock Collection*

A more interesting acquisition from the Red Rover fleet was DAU358C, a Weymann bodied AEC Renown. It is seen here sporting the livery of its former owner. *D.J. Hancock Collection*

Between 1986 and 1988, Luton & District took stock of a number of Iveco 49.10 minibuses with either Robin Hood or Dormobile bodywork. 78 (E349DRO) is seen representing the type, carrying Dormobile bodywork. New to the company in July 1988, it is seen wearing the Hoppanstopper livery. *D.J. Hancock Collection*

Luton railway station provides the backdrop of Leyland Lynx 410 (H410ERO). Four such vehicles were taken into stock in October 1990 at Luton to operate a shuttle service between Luton railway station and Luton Airport, branded as the 'Luton Flyer'. For this service, the vehicles wore a dedicated livery, as can be seen in this view. *Gary Seamarks*

A number of Leyland Atlanteans originating with London Country Bus Services were taken into stock when the operations of London Country (North West) were acquired by Luton & District in October 1990. Representing the Park Royal bodied Atlanteans is AN170 (XPG170T), seen having just left Slough bus station, bound for Langley. *Peter Johnson Collection/D.J. Hancock Collection*

100 Leyland National saloons entered the Luton & District fleet when London Country (North West) was acquired by the company. Representing this large batch is SNB398 (YPL398T) seen in Slough town centre, approaching the Bus Station. *Peter Johnson Collection/D.J. Hancock Collection*

New to London Country Bus Services was B291KPF. It was acquired through London Country (North West), and is seen wearing the livery of its new owners. Buckingham Palace Road, Victoria provides the location of this photograph. *D.J. Hancock Collection*

The acquisition of London Country (North West) in October 1990 saw the introduction of five Reeve Burgess bodied Dodge S56 minibuses to the fleet. D682NVS was originally numbered MBD21 by its previous owners. It is seen in Luton wearing a revised Hoppanstopper livery. *Gary Seamarks*

Several London Regional Transport contracts were acquired with the business of London Country (North West), including the 142 (Watford Junction – Brent Cross). Edgware bus station finds LR81 (G281UMJ), a Leyland bodied Leyland Olympian, operating a 142 towards Brent Cross. The non-red operators were required to display a London Regional Transport sticker on the front, near-side of the vehicle as seen here. *Peter Johnson Collection/D.J. Hancock Collection*

Seven coaches were acquired from Lee & District in October 1990, a subsidiary of London Country (North West). NJF204W was allotted rolling stock number LD1, being the only example to be renumbered by The Shires, as 1205. This Plaxton bodied Bedford YMQ is seen wearing the livery of its previous owner. *Gary Seamarks*

February 1991 saw the arrival of eight Carlyle bodied Dennis Dart saloons for the former London Country operation. DC8 (H245MUK) represents the batch, showing the livery worn by buses operating from the former London Country (North West) garages. This particular example was allocated to Hemel Hempstead, with Hemel Bus fleet names just visible on the side. *D.J. Hancock Collection*

Another view of the Hoppanstopper livery is seen here, applied to 11 (F128TRU), a Reeve Burgess bodied Mercedes-Benz 709D. Six vehicles of this type were taken into stock by Luton & District in August 1988. *Gary Seamarks*

Ten Talbot Pullman minibuses arrived from East Midland Motor Services Ltd, Mansfield in April 1992. They entered service wearing the Stagecoach stripe livery, with Luton & District fleet names being applied. Seen at Castle Street, Luton is D81RVM and another example of the type. *Gary Seamarks*

August 1992 saw the arrival of five ECW bodied Bristol VRTs from Lincoln City Transport. 25 (LFE25P) was new to its former operator in December 1975. It is seen wearing its former operator's livery and fleet number, with a modest Luton & District fleet name applied just above the front windscreen. *Gary Seamarks*

Twenty Northern Counties bodied Volvo B6 saloons arrived with Luton & District in September 1994. 332 (M712OMJ) was allocated to Luton. It is seen wearing the new yellow, blue and grey livery introduced under the reformed The Shires. It clearly shows the disadvantage of the dot-matrix destination displays fitted to many buses. *Gary Seamarks*

A pair of ECW bodied Leyland Olympians were taken into stock by Luton & District in November 1994 from Rhonda Buses Ltd, Porth. MUH284X was originally numbered 600 but was later renumbered 5064. It is this fleet number that the vehicle can be seen displaying in this shot at Aylesbury garage. *Gary Seamarks*

February 1995 saw the arrival of five Made-to-Measure bodied Mercedes-Benz 609D minibuses from the Birmingham Omnibus Company Ltd, Tividale. 17 (K27WND) is seen heading towards Luton town centre, showing off the yellow and blue livery of The Shires, along with the Luton & Dunstable fleet names. *Gary Seamarks*

A quartet of ECW bodied Bristol VRTs were acquired in August 1995 from Crosville Motors Ltd, along with a pair of Leyland National saloons. UDM448V was originally number 978 by The Shires, it survived with the company long enough to be renumbered. It is seen operating a school journey whilst carrying its new number 5036. *Gary Seamarks*

During 1995 a number of National Greenways vehicles were acquired from Crosville Cymru. Initially allocated to High Wycombe, they later found use from other garages. 3045 (IIL4822) is seen loading in Leighton Buzzard High Street. The Aylesbury operation used the fleet name Aylesbury & the Vale. *Matt Robinson*

Church Street, Luton finds Leyland National 2 591 (GUW461W) which the company acquired from Parfitts Motor Services of Rhymney Bridge. The vehicle itself was new to London Transport as LS461. The relaunch of the company in 1995 saw the introduction of a new livery which can be seen being worn by 591. *Gary Seamarks*

Fourteen Plaxton Beaver bodied Mercedes-Benz 709D minibuses were delivered to The Shires in September and October 1995. N911ETM was part of this batch, originally numbered MP261 it was renumbered 2131 in 1997. Luton's Bute Street Bus Station finds this vehicle on layover wearing the Arriva corporate livery. *David Beddall*

1996 saw many new vehicles enter the fleet, including ten Northern Counties bodied Volvo Olympians at Luton. ON041 (N41JPP) is seen departing Luton town centre, whilst operating a journey on route 27. *Gary Seamarks*

Two batches of East Lancs European bodied Scania L113CRL saloons were delivered to The Shires in 1995 and 1996. 718 (N29KGS) arrived in June 1996. It is seen carrying Sapphire branding for Luton town service 31 between the town centre and Dunstable. *Gary Seamarks*

The Shires acquired the business of Lucketts of Watford in January 1997. This brought with it a varied collection of vehicles including two Marshall bodied Dennis Darts. Showing off the type is L400BUS which was given rolling stock number 3104. It is seen paused at Milton Keynes rail station. *Liam Farrer-Beddall*

Nine Plaxton Paladin bodied Scania L113CRL saloons arrived with The Shires during October 1997. 3198 (R198RBM) represents this small batch, whilst loading in Central Milton Keynes. *David Beddall*

Originally new to the company in January 1998 for Luton's Green Line service 757, 4051 (R451SKX) was later reallocated to Hemel Hempstead to operate Green Line route 758 between the town and London Victoria. Marble Arch sees 4051 heading back to Hemel Hempstead, sporting branding for the service. *Liam Farrer-Beddall*

January 1998 saw the arrival of ten Plaxton Pointer bodied Dennis Dart SLF saloons with Arriva the Shires at Garston for local services. 3209 (R209GMJ) shows off the styling of this type, wearing a newer version of the Arriva livery. It is seen passing through Watford town centre before embarking on a journey to Hemel Hempstead. *Liam Farrer-Beddall*

The Shires acquired the business of Lutonian Buses in March 1998, inheriting a number of Iveco minibuses. Dating back to 1996 was N124GNM, a Carlyle bodied Iveco 59-12. Under the control of The Shires, four-digit fleet numbers were applied to the Lutonian fleet, with this vehicle gaining rolling stock number 2214. It is seen parked at Bute Street bus station. *David Beddall*

2185 (R185DNM), a Plaxton Beaver 2 bodied Mercedes-Benz O810 minibus, was part of a batch of fourteen similar vehicles delivered to Arriva the Shires in April 1998, and again were allocated to a number of garages. 2185 is seen parked at Stevenage bus station. *Liam Farrer-Beddall*

Both Garston and Aylesbury benefitted from the 1998 delivery of Northern Counties Palatine II bodied Volvo Olympians. Those at Aylesbury were put to use on route 280 between the town and Oxford, for which the vehicles were branded. 5157 (S157KNK) is seen here approaching Oxford railway station, having just completed a journey in from Aylesbury. The route branding can be seen clearly in this view. *Gary Seamarks*

Seven Alexander Dash bodied Volvo B6 saloons arrived from Arriva Scotland West during 1998. 3244 (M844DDS) represents the type, seen travelling along St Peters Street, St Albans whilst operating a journey on route 300. *David Beddall*

Arriva the Shires took stock of a number of Van Hool Alizee bodied DAF SB3000 coaches from Grey Green during 1998 to upgrade some of the fleet on express work. 4060 (M948LYR) was one such example and is seen starting its journey to London Victoria, having just left Stevenage bus station. *David Beddall*

A fleet of twenty-five Marshall C31 bodied Iveco 59-12 minibuses were taken into stock from Arriva East Herts & Essex in October 1998. 2339 (M719UTW) is seen here, representing the batch wearing County Bus livery. *D.J. Hancock Collection*

Six Wright Handybus bodied Dennis Dart saloons were acquired from County Bus & Coach in October 1998. 3352 (J402XVX) is seen parked at Stevenage bus station in between duties on local service 2. *David Beddall*

LR10 (TPD110X) was inherited in October 1990 from London Country (North West). Numbered 5380 by The Shires in 1997, this vehicle was put to use as a staff rest room at Watford Junction. It is seen here in this guise. *David Beddall*

Nineteen Alexander ALX200 bodied Dennis Dart SLF saloons were purchased during May 2000 to upgrade Transport for London services in the Walthamstow area of London, operated from Debden garage. W476XKX formed part of this batch, originally numbered 3476. These Darts later passed to Arriva London, who renumbered them as ADLs, with 3476 becoming ADL76. It is seen passing through Hackney Central. *Liam Farrer-Beddall*

A smaller number of the longer Alexander ALX300 models were purchased in 2000 by Arriva the Shires on the Volvo B10BLE chassis. 3452 (W452XKX) is seen here loading at Stevenage Bus Station. They were initially purchased for use on local services, denoted by the route branding applied. *David Beddall*

The Arriva the Shires group received twenty-seven Alexander ALX400 bodied Dennis Tridents during 2000, split between Luton and Southend. Luton received twelve such vehicles for route 38. The last of these, 5433 (W433XKX), is seen loading in Luton town centre, off route. Route branding was applied to these vehicles as can be seen. *David Beddall*

Seventeen Plaxton Pointer MPD bodied Dennis Dart SLF saloons were taken into stock by Arriva the Shires in July 2000. 3494 (W494YGS) was a member of this batch, and is seen approaching Stevenage bus station. *D.J. Hancock Collection*

High Wycombe's bus station finds 3821 (N521MJO), a Plaxton Pointer bodied Dennis Dart SLF saloon inherited by Arriva the Shires in December 2000 from the Wycombe Bus Company. It is seen wearing a revised version of the Arriva corporate livery for a High Wycombe local service. *David Beddall*

April 2001 saw the arrival of five Optare Solo saloons at Aylesbury garage where they were put to use on local services. 0442 (Y42HBT) is seen here wearing a green livery complete with 'Rainbow Routes' branding. *David Beddall*

Arriva the Shires started a new service between Biggleswade and Potton, serving villages in the local area. For this a pair of Optare Aleros were taken into stock at Hitchin. YS51HDN represents the pair and is seen passing through the ford in the village of Sutton. *Nick Doolan*

London routes 142 and 340 were restocked with new vehicles in 2002 with the arrival of twenty-four Transbus ALX400 bodied VDL DB250s. Watford Junction finds 6021 (KL52CXO) wearing the London 'cow horn' livery, showing off its two-doored layout. *David Beddall*

4519 (KE03OUN) was one of seven Wright Cadet bodied VDL SB120 saloons taken into stock by Arriva the Shires in April 2003 and allocated to a number of garages. 4519 was added to the Stevenage allocation and is seen on layover at Bute Street Bus Station, Luton having just completed a journey on route 101. *David Beddall*

A more unusual type to operate with The Shires was the Alexander PS bodied Volvo B10M. Only three examples were operated by the company, all acquired from Sovereign in January 2005. 3331 (M782PRS) is seen loading in St Albans city centre having gained a full repaint into Arriva livery. *David Beddall*

Fifty-three vehicles were taken into stock from the Sovereign operation, expanding Arriva's presence in Stevenage. 3303 (W131XRO) was one of sixteen Wright Renown bodied Volvo B10BLEs acquired. It is seen loading in St Peters Street, St Albans wearing the Arriva interurban livery, whilst carrying branding for Centraline routes 300/301. *David Beddall*

Another example of the Wright Renown bodied Volvo B10BLE saloons taken into stock from Sovereign is 3313 (PN02HVM). It is seen at Stevenage bus station wearing the livery of its former owner. These vehicles were taken into stock wearing route branding for Stevenage town route SB1. *David Beddall*

A handful of coaches were also acquired from Sovereign. Plaxton bodied Dennis Javelin 4029 (M101CCD) was one of them. It is seen wearing Green Line livery for route 797 (Stevenage-Hatfield-London), having just departed Stevenage bus station.
David Beddall

Seven Wright Eclipse Urban bodied Volvo B7RLE saloons were added to High Wycombe's allocation in February and March 2005 for use on local services. The penultimate member of the batch, 3866 (KE05FMO), is seen departing High Wycombe bus station destined for Penn. *Liam Farrer-Beddall*

Nineteen Wright
Solar bodied Scania L94UB saloons were taken into stock between September and November 2005 at Luton to modernise the fleet used on town services 27 and 38. As can be seen in the photograph, route branding was applied to the vehicles. 3609 (KE55GVZ) was branded for route 38 (Luton-Houghton Regis-Dunstable). However, it is seen off route, on layover in Central Milton Keynes, with the infamous Xscape building visible in the right-hand side. *David Beddall*

Luton's Green Line 757 saw investment in new coaches a number of times in the 2000s, with older rolling stock being pushed out to other garages, upgrading the fleet there. 4066 (YJ55WSV) formed part of a batch of five Van Hool Alizee bodied VDL SB4000 coaches originally taken into stock for the 757 and were the first wheelchair accessible coaches in the fleet. When newer Van Hool coaches were received at Luton in 2009, some were reallocated to Stevenage for use on the 797. 4066 is seen at Norton Green Road garage, branded for route 797 (Stevenage-Hatfield-London). *David Beddall*

The Optare Versa was taken into stock in a small quantity by Arriva the Shires. The first two examples were allocated to High Wycombe. 2402 (YJ57EKG) is seen on local Orange Route 39 to Hicks Farm Rise. As can be seen in this photograph, 2402 wore an appropriate livery and route branding. *David Beddall*

September to November 2008 saw the arrival of numerous Mercedes-Benz Citaro saloons at Garston and Aylesbury. Garston employed their Citaros on the 321, whilst Aylesbury used theirs on route 300 between the town and High Wycombe. However, they often strayed onto other services as demonstrated above. 3922 (BK58URP) is seen in Central Milton Keynes loading for route 100 back to Aylesbury. *Liam Farrer-Beddall*

Route 280 (Aylesbury-Oxford) gained a fleet of Enviro 400s in November 2008. One such example was 5453 (SN58ENY) seen here in Oxford city centre, heading back towards Aylesbury. The fleet underwent a refurbishment program to upgrade the fleet to Sapphire specification. It is in this livery that we see it. *Liam Farrer-Beddall*

Sixteen Van Hool T917 Alicron coaches were taken into stock at Luton over the course of 2008 and 2009. 4380 (YJ58FKA) was delivered in December 2008 along with twelve others to take up service on the 757 (Luton Airport-London Victoria). The majority wore Green Line livery, with a couple gaining full Easybus livery. 4380 is seen on layover at Luton Airport. *David Beddall*

The MK Metro operation took stock of seven Caetano Levante bodied Scania K340EB4 coaches in June 2009 after winning the contract for two further routes. 0420 (FJ09DXL) is seen here heading for Northampton's bus station before entering service. *Liam Farrer-Beddall*

Routes 300 and 301 were upgraded in 2009 with the arrival of a batch of ADL Enviro 300 saloons in June. Representing these vehicles is 3555 (KX09GYE), seen loading in St Albans city centre. Less obvious route branding was applied to these vehicles. *Liam Farrer-Beddall*

September 2009 saw a pair of Wrightbus Integral Gemini 2 double-decks delivered to Garston to assist with an increase in the PVR on Transport for London routes. 6101 (KX59AEF) is seen passing Harrow bus station bound for South Harrow on route 258. *Liam Farrer-Beddall*

YJ55KZS, a DAF SB3000 complete with Van Hool Alizee bodywork, was new to Arriva Midland Fox for National Express contracts. When these contracts were transferred across to Arriva MK Metro, the coaches came too. The loss of some of these contracts saw the coaches put to use on Green Line routes into the capital. Allocated rolling stock number 4070, this vehicle was later added to Hemel Hempstead's allocation and used on route 758. *Liam Farrer-Beddall*

S651KJU, a Northern Counties bodied Volvo Olympian, arrived with The Shires in May 2010 from Arriva Midlands, numbered 5162. It was allocated to High Wycombe where it was captured by the camera. *Liam Farrer-Beddall*

A pair of Caetano Levante bodied Scania K340EB6 coaches were received in April and May 2012 from Classic Coaches, Annfield Plain. 4201 (FJ08KMG) was the second example received in May at Luton. They were put to use on the 757, repainted into Green Livery with an Easybus rear. This livery can be clearly seen as 4201 crosses the junction of Marylebone Road and Baker Street. *Liam Farrer-Beddall*

In October 2012, the ALX400 bodied DAF DB250s operating routes 142 and 340 in North London were replaced by sixteen similar bodied Volvo B7TLs from Arriva London, with the DB250s being cascaded around The Shires for further use. 6168 (LJ55BVW) is seen entering Edgware bus station whilst heading for Watford Junction on route 142. These vehicles later transferred back to Arriva London, regaining their VLA class codes. *Liam Farrer-Beddall*

The Volvo B7TLs were not the only second-hand double-deckers received from Arriva London. A number of DAF DB250s complete with ALX400 bodywork were taken into stock by Arriva the Shires over a number of years. High Wycombe finds 6300 (Y524UGC) which was taken into stock in November 2013. *Liam Farrer-Beddall*

Garston's route
10 was upgraded in 2013 when ten Optare Versa saloons arrived with the company in January. 3419 (KX62JPY) is seen stopped in Watford town centre, showing off the more subtle route branding applied to these vehicles.
Liam Farrer-Beddall

Seven MCV
Evolution bodied MAN 14.220 saloons arrived from Tellings Golden Miller in the spring of 2013. They were allocated to High Wycombe from where they were put to use on route 1. 3741 (AE06OPG) is seen carrying this branding, departing the town's bus station.
Liam Farrer-Beddall

Thirteen Wright
Eclipse Urban bodied Volvo B7RLE saloons were taken into stock at Luton and Hemel Hempstead in September and October 2013. 3968 (LT63UNM) was one allocated to Hemel Hempstead, where they were used on town service 2, gaining branding for the service as can be seen above.
Liam Farrer-Beddall

Milton Keynes
garage took stock of the only all-electric Wrightbus Streetlite minibuses in 2013/2014. These vehicles stand out from the conventional diesel versions of the Streetlite, by the addition of the dome on the roof. 5006 (KP63TEO) is seen loading in Central Milton Keynes before it heads to Wolverton. Note the images of the batteries at the rear of the vehicle.
Liam Farrer-Beddall

A pair of Wrightbus Streetlite WFs were initially taken on loan by Arriva the Shires at Milton Keynes to help support the fleet of similar electric vehicles. They were later taken into stock, wearing a silver livery. HRZ6499 was allocated rolling stock number 0449. It is seen heading to Bletchley passing Milton Keynes Theatre District.
Liam Farrer-Beddall

Four Caetano Levante bodied Volvo B9R coaches arrived in December 2014 from Tellings Golden Miller, after the loss of some National Express contracts. They were repainted into Green Line livery and used on the 757. 4101 (FJ60HYH) is seen on layover at Luton Interchange showing off how smart these vehicles looked in Green Line livery.
Liam Farrer-Beddall

Town services in Luton were given new rolling stock in the early part of 2015 when a fleet of Wrightbus Streetlite WFs were taken into stock. To promote how environmentally friendly the fleet were, a revised green livery was applied. 2513 (LM64JNZ) is seen here operating a journey on route 29 to Farley Hill having just loaded passengers at Luton Interchange. *Liam Farrer-Beddall*

The opening months of 2015 saw twenty Wright bodied VDL SB200 saloons arrive from Arriva Merseyside, allocated to Stevenage and Milton Keynes. 3771 (MX12KXA) was one allocated to Milton Keynes in March. The Milton Keynes batch were put to use on cross town service 6 (Wolverton-Stony Stratford-CMK-Bletchley) and repainted into Sapphire Livery as can be seen above. *Liam Farrer-Beddall*

Plaxton Pointer
MPD bodied Dennis Dart SLF 3288 (Y383HKE) was acquired from Arriva Midlands to replace similar non-DDA compliant saloons. It is seen at Dunstable town centre having just completed a journey in from Aylesbury on route 61.
Liam Farrer-Beddall

Arriva Midlands transferred numerous examples of the rarer East Lancs Myllennium Lowlander bodied DAF DB250 double-deck to The Shires. 4712 (FE51YWK) arrived with the company in July 2016, being allocated to Luton, with others being allocated to Aylesbury. Dunstable town centre provides the backdrop to this photograph.
Liam Farrer-Beddall

Thirty-five AD E20/ Enviro 200 MMC saloons were ordered by Arriva Midlands in 2017, with all but four of them being allocated to Arriva the Shires. Luton, High Wycombe and Milton Keynes took stock of these vehicles for town services. Above we see 3123 (YX17NPF) loading in Central Milton Keynes, whilst 3130 (YX17NNF) is seen below in Luton town centre. The new Sapphire livery was applied to those allocated to Milton Keynes, along with route branding. The Luton and High Wycombe fleet wore the new standard corporate livery. *Liam Farrer-Beddall*

Another vehicle acquired from Arriva Midlands was 2297 (BF52NZP), a Plaxton Pointer MPD bodied Dennis Dart SLF. It is seen paused at Milton Keynes Rail Station whilst operating a local service. *Liam Farrer-Beddall*

Twelve Wrightbus Streetlite DF saloons were transferred to Milton Keynes from Arriva Midlands. 3340 (FJ64JYL) is seen here heading for the Westcroft Centre, leaving Milton Keynes rail station. *Liam Farrer-Beddall*

The introduction of new coaches on the 757 Green Line service in 2017 also saw a revised livery applied to them. Thirteen Mercedes-Benz Tourismo coaches were purchased by Arriva the Shires for use on the service, wearing a white based livery. 7002 (BP17URK) is seen negotiating Hyde Park Corner. *Liam Farrer-Beddall*

A handful of Wright Eclipse Gemini bodied Volvo B7TLs were acquired from Arriva Midlands and allocated to Aylesbury. 4018 (UUI2910) is seen approaching Aylesbury bus station. *Liam Farrer-Beddall*

Above: **October 2019** saw the delivery of six Temsa Safari coaches to Luton. It was intended that they would replace 9000-9003 on the 758 Green Line service between Hemel Hempstead and London Victoria. However, these vehicles were slow in entering service, none of which did so until 2020. Representing the batch is 7104 (YJ69AAY), captured by the camera departing Hemel Hempstead bound for London Victoria on the 758. *Hazel Richardson*

Opposite above: **November 2019** saw the arrival of HX04HTY, a Caetano Nimbus bodied Transbus Dart. It was acquired from Arriva Kent Thameside and added to the driver training fleet, gaining rolling stock number T946. It is seen on layover in Hemel Hempstead. *Hazel Richardson*

Opposite below: **January 2020** saw the arrival of a solitary Optare Versa from Arriva Midlands. 2991 (YJ09MKE) was allocated to Luton, where it is seen on layover at the town's transport interchange. It is seen wearing the new Arriva livery. *Liam Farrer-Beddall*

Above: **Milton Keynes** railway station finds Mercedes-Benz Sprinter 1015 (BF67WGN) whilst on loan to the company as a crew ferry. It is seen wearing the new Arriva corporate livery. 1015 was soon replaced by sister vehicle 1003 from Luton. *David Beddall*

Opposite above: **The Covid-19** pandemic of 2020 saw the double-decking of some of Milton Keynes busy services, this including the 300. 4210 (FJ58KXH) was one of a number of Wright Eclipse Gemini bodied Volvo B9TLs to transfer to Arriva the Shires from Arriva Midlands. It is seen operating the 300 departing Milton Keynes Station. *Liam Farrer-Beddall*

Opposite below: **At the** same time, a fleet of Wright Eclipse Urban bodied Volvo B7RLEs were also transferred to Milton Keynes from Arriva Midlands. 3903 (FJ58HYM) is seen departing the town's rail station operating a local service. *Liam Farrer-Beddall*

A fleet of Mercedes-Benz Tourismo coaches were ordered for a new Green Line service between Liverpool Street and Stanstead Airport. The onset of Covid-19 saw the route delayed in starting. In August 2020, a number of them were placed in service from Luton for the 755 and 757 services. 7203 (BV20HRE) is seen approaching Luton Airport wearing the revised Green Line livery. *Liam Farrer-Beddall*

Three VDL saloons were hired from Arriva Bus & Coach during the early part of 2020. YJ58FFA is seen operating Luton route 27, passing the University of Bedfordshire. This vehicle was allocated rolling stock number 3812. *Liam Farrer-Beddall*

BIBLIOGRAPHY

A fleet history of Luton Corporation Transport; PSV Circle; 2012

Birch Bros. Ltd: On the move; The Rotary Club of Rushden Chichele

Cook, Robert, *Red Rover Bus Company*, Tempus Publishing; 2007

Crawley, R.J., MacGregor, D.R., Simpson, F.D., *The Years Between 1909 and 1969: Vols 1 and 2: The National Story to 1929*; Oxford Publishing Co.; 1979 & 1984

Cummings, J.M., *London's Forgotten Bus Operations: Public Motor Transport in Bedfordshire 1899-1919*; London Historical Research Group; 1994

Rose, Peter, *Luton Corporation Transport*, The History Press; 2009

Warwick, Roger M., *An Illustrated History of United Counties Omnibus Company Limited: Parts 6-17*